## Praise for Tavis Smiley

"You have Oprah and you have Tavis—they are the king and queen."
—*The New York Times*

"Arguably the nation's most influential black journalist."
—*USA Today*

"Smiley is one of the most important political voices of his generation."
—*The Philadelphia Inquirer*

"Smiley is a reminder of the days when talk show hosts were conversationalists, not sycophants or joke meters."
—*Los Angeles Times*

"Look out Larry King—here comes Tavis Smiley!"
—*The New York Post*

"One of the most dynamic, outside-the-lines voices in American journalism."
—*Austin American-Statesman*

"[Tavis Smiley] provides one place that helps promote dialogues that might not otherwise take place before audiences who might not otherwise think that they have anything in common."
—*New York Daily News*

"Clear, passionate, and to the point. . . . [Smiley] gives you the impression he's a friend talking directly to you."
—*Detroit Free Press*

"In the age of high-decibel, in-your-face talk shows, Tavis Smiley keeps the volume low and the content high." —*The Plain Dealer*

# Tavis Smiley

## What I Know for Sure

Tavis Smiley is the host of *Tavis Smiley* on PBS and *The Tavis Smiley Show* with PRI (Public Radio International). Named by *Newsweek* as one of the "20 people changing how Americans get their news" and singled out by *Time* as one of America's most promising young leaders, he is the author of the bestsellers *Hard Left*, *Doing What's Right*, *How to Make Black America Better*, and *Keeping the Faith*. He lives in Los Angeles.

David Ritz has written biographies of, among others, Ray Charles, Marvin Gaye, Aretha Franklin, and B.B. King. His latest book, *Messengers: Portraits of African American Ministers, Evangelists, Gospel Singers, and Other Messengers of the Word*, was published by Doubleday in 2006.

"*And if there is a victory, it will be a victory not merely for fifty thousand Negroes but a victory for justice and the forces of light.*"

MARTIN LUTHER KING JR.,
*speaking to the people of Montgomery, Alabama*

# What I Know for Sure

MY STORY OF GROWING UP IN AMERICA

## Tavis Smiley

### with David Ritz

Anchor Books
A Division of Random House, Inc.
New York

For Phyllis

FIRST ANCHOR BOOKS EDITION, JANUARY 2008

*Copyright © 2006 by Tavis Smiley*

All rights reserved. Published in the United States by Anchor Books,
a division of Random House, Inc., New York, and in Canada by
Random House of Canada Limited, Toronto. *What I Know for Sure*
was originally published in hardcover in the United States by Doubleday,
an imprint of The Doubleday Broadway Publishing Group, a division
of Random House, Inc., New York, in 2006.

Anchor Books and colophon are registered trademarks of
Random House, Inc.

The Cataloging-in-Publication Data is on file at the Library of Congress.

**Anchor ISBN: 978-0-385-72172-1**

*Book design by Gretchen Achilles*

www.anchorbooks.com

Printed in the United States of America
10  9  8  7  6  5  4  3  2  1

# Contents

## Contents

# Acknowledgments

This year, two thousand and six, marks my tenth year working with Roger Scholl, the only book editor I've ever had. I'm grateful to Roger and to Doubleday for a decade of allowing me to express myself.

As you'll read on the pages that follow, loyalty is paramount for me. In my entire professional career, I've had only one editor, one partner, one lawyer, one business manager, and one accountant. Roger, Denise, Ken, Harold, and Errol still serve in those capacities.

This year also marks my fifteenth year in the media broadcast business, and I'm fortunate that these friends have been with me every step of the way. Through the hirings and the firings, the bestsellers and the no-sellers, the critical acclaim and the searing criticism.

I've been more fortunate; I've been blessed beyond measure.

Throughout the book, you'll come to understand how faith, family, and friends have sustained me.

In the end, if this book is about anything it is about this one thing I know for sure: LOVE WINS.

So, to all those persons who have ever worked with me, for me, or around me; to all those persons who have ever inspired me, supported me, or prayed for me; to all those persons who have ever enlightened me, encouraged me, or empowered me—I acknowledge YOU.

# Introduction

This isn't a formal autobiography or a definitive memoir. I feel to attempt such a work while still in my early forties would be presumptuous.

Having said that, I've consciously tried to write a narrative about the experiences that have helped shape the person I have become. With every page, I've tried to answer a simple question: What have I learned that might help others?

In revisiting the turning points in my life, I am comforted by those words of Socrates that my dear friend and mentor Dr. Cornel West never tires of quoting: "The unexamined life is not worth living." Writing this book has certainly helped me to reexamine my own life.

As people who know me well can attest, I take pride in writing my own speeches and commentaries for radio and television. But I don't consider myself a storyteller. So in writing this book I sought the assistance of a collaborator who could listen to me with an objective ear and help me craft a narrative that would be compelling and, I hope, insightful. That is why I turned to David Ritz. I've known David Ritz for several years, in part through his work with Marvin Gaye, Ray Charles, Aretha Franklin, and B. B. King, among others; I feel honored to be in such distinguished company.

David and I have worked chronologically because that seemed the simplest way to tell my story, to re-create the formative years of my childhood, teen years, college experience, and entry into the world of government and media. In reexamining my life on the page, I have struggled to weigh the impact of church, race, family, class, culture, and politics on my values and character.

If my relative young age made me wary of writing a memoir, I came to see its advantage: the traumas and dramas of my younger years are, perhaps, fresher in my mind. We have tried to ensure that the images and language we employ reflect that freshness.

When Moses asked God to define himself, God said, "I Am the I Am." There is nothing, God said, but the present; past and future are illusions. In that same spirit, Dr. King described such influences as "forces of light." I can think of no better phrase. The reconciliation of my past with my present life and faith is an ongoing process. Those forces that informed me as a youth continue to do so today. They defy linear thinking. They defy gravity. I believe such lessons and memories are not merely the miracles that get us through difficult times in our lives but are powerful tools that reinforce our spirit here and now, every second of every day.

If I am able to recount those forces of light in my life, it is only because the Source of that light, the source of all creativity, has guided me. That same Source has guided the writing of this book.

So it is with deep humility and love that I offer thanks and praise to the Source of all that is good.

# Gulfport to Gotham

When I listen to Stevie Wonder's brilliant song about New York City, "Living for the City," my mind goes back to Mama. You'll remember that in the song, when the singing stops, a small drama begins: A Mississippi native takes the bus heading north, arriving in the midst of the great metropolis. Getting off the bus, he exclaims, "New York, just like I pictured it, skyscrapers and everything!"

I imagine my mother as that Mississippian.

When she took the bus from Gulfport, Mississippi, in 1964, I was with her, inside her womb.

That's where my story begins . . .

My mama, Joyce Marie Roberts, was stunningly beautiful. At eighteen, she exuded energy and confidence. But she also harbored a burdensome secret: she was pregnant. Her mother was a devout Christian who raised her and her brother and two sisters in the St.

James Baptist Church of Gulfport, Mississippi, where the pastor preached fire and brimstone. Being pregnant was not part of the Baptist Church plan.

Mama had been a dutiful daughter, helping her mother, who worked six, sometimes seven days a week as a maid. Her daddy had a good job as a longshoreman. But my grandfather was known for drinking. As a result, Mama's family was always scuffling.

Mama shined in school. She was far more than just a green-eyed beauty; she was also a gifted athlete, excelling at basketball and track. Later, I heard stories about how she invigorated the pep squad with her tireless energy, and how she led the school band as they marched through downtown Gulfport during homecoming weekend. From all accounts, she loved life.

Mama was also a James Brown fanatic. When Brown came to Mississippi to perform, she perched herself in the front row, and as J.B. broke into his "mashed potato," slipping and sliding from one side of the stage to the other, Mama held on to his leg and wouldn't let go. Lord, Mama could party, and she loved to laugh. While still in high school, she fell in love with one of the school's star basketball players, a boy I'll call T.

After graduating from Thirty-third Avenue High School, she worked at the Gulfport Laundry and Gates Cleaners, helping her mother with household expenses. But Mama always had an adventuresome spirit, and an advertisement in the local paper caught her eye. An employment agency was seeking young women as sleep-in maids in private homes in New York City. Displaying her independent streak and her courage, Mama signed up with the agency, and caught a bus up to New York City. Unfortunately, she was only there briefly; an injury sustained in a car accident sent her back home only a few months later. Upon her return to Gulfport, she and T renewed their romance. The result was my conception.

Mama didn't want to stay in Gulfport and face the scandal her pregnancy would cause. She didn't want her mother to know her condition. So she went back to the agency that had originally sent her to New York and took a job up north on Long Island, working again as a maid. But she also knew she needed to find a man to marry, to make me legitimate. She met a man named Scott, a West Indian, who wanted to get married to stay in America. So out of convenience, Joyce married Scott, something I didn't learn until I was an adult.

Months later, she realized she had made a mistake. Homesick and lonely for her own mother, Mama decided to go back to Gulfport, alone, to have her baby.

## Gotham to Gulfport

When the bus pulled into Gulfport, Mama saw her mother waiting. Mama was exhausted from the long journey, and she was plagued by doubt and shame. Seven months pregnant, she was as big as a barn. What would her mother say?

After embracing, her mother held her gaze, telling her, "I always knew the truth. Your daddy told me. He had heard it through your friends. Believe me, it doesn't matter. We love you and we're happy you're home. Jesus said that he didn't come to judge. Well, if he's not in the judging business, neither am I."

And with that, Mama wept in her mother's arms.

I was born on September 13, 1964, in Gulfport, a little over two weeks after the Mississippi Freedom Democratic Party, led by Fannie Lou Hamer, appeared on the floor of the Democratic National

Convention in Atlantic City to challenge the state's all-white representation.

After my birth, Mama and I lived with her mother.

T, the eighteen-year-old boy who'd fathered me, came 'round to see Mama, hoping to repair their relationship. They had several dates and, to some degree, they continued to be attracted to each other. T accompanied Mama to the movies, to the candy store, even to the doctor when it was time for my checkup. T didn't know that Mama was already married. When he found out, accompanying my mother to see a lawyer about a divorce, he was floored. In the end, Mama went her way, and T went his.

In 1965, a year after I was born—the same year that Martin Luther King Jr. and his supporters walked down U.S. 80 from Selma, Alabama, to Montgomery—my Mama met Emory Garnell Smiley. The march took four days and changed the course of American history. My mother's introduction to Emory Smiley would change my family history.

Mama first met Garnell, the man I would know as my father, on a double date with a girlfriend. Garnell and the other man were in the air force, stationed in nearby Biloxi. That night, at the drive-in, Mama and Emory Garnell Smiley sat together in the backseat.

As the second movie began, the couple in front started to neck.

"Would you like to walk to the refreshment stand?" Smiley asked, noticing Mama's discomfort.

"Yes," Mama replied gratefully.

After buying Mama a candy bar, he led her to a bench behind the last row of cars.

"We could just sit here and talk," he suggested.

"How long have you been in the air force?" asked Mama.

"Not long."

"You come from around here?"

"No, from Georgia. Little town called Midway."

"So, your daddy in the armed services too?"

"No, Daddy's a truck driver for a pulp mill. Worked there his whole life."

"You've lived there your whole life?"

"Yep, until I went to New York."

"You lived in New York City?"

"Sure did."

"Me, too," said Mama. "Been there twice."

"I wasn't too crazy about New York," admitted Garnell.

"Me either. What made you go up there?"

"Oh, I don't know. You hear about the big city and you think you better see it. You think you're missing something."

"That's how I felt," said Mama.

"I worked at a hospital in Brooklyn as an orderly. I was looking for some formal training that would get me a better job, but they weren't interested in training. So I joined the air force. Right now I'm training to repair planes. What were you doing up in New York?"

"I was working as a nanny. Then I went back a second time to . . . well, to have my baby."

"I didn't know you had a baby."

"Well, you know now," says Joyce.

"I love babies. Boy or girl?"

"Boy. His name is Tavis."

"Good name. And his daddy?"

"Not really in my life right now. I'm not sure why I'm telling you all this," said Mama, "except I'm comfortable talking to you. You're easy to talk to."

"I feel the same about you," said Garnell. "I like how you don't hide things. So many women feel like they gotta play a man."

"I like that you're serious-minded, Garnell."

"My daddy took responsibility for his family. He's taught me to do the same. I was raised an only child, but not long ago Mama and Daddy adopted two orphan girls and cared for them like their own. Now they're my sisters."

"Your mama work?"

"She's a beautician. Works at a funeral parlor. She fixes the hair of ladies who've passed on. She also plays piano in the parlor."

"My daddy works at the dock. Makes good money; but on payday, you can't get him out of the bar room."

"I know what that's like. On the same property as our house, Daddy built a juke joint with his own hands. Calls it Smiley's Place. Nothing fancy: milk crates as chairs, Mama's homemade fish and chicken. We have an old jukebox filled with the blues. But folks love to come over after work to drink and relax. At night, there's dancing."

"I love to dance," said Mama.

"I'd love to dance with you," Garnell replied, surprising himself with his boldness.

She looked in his eyes and saw reflected in them a man of purpose. Garnell Smiley conveyed an air of trust; something about him said, *I'll be loyal to you no matter what.*

The next year, 1966, the year Dr. King initiated his Chicago Campaign for open housing, Stokely Carmichael promoted Black Power, and James Meredith was shot in the back by a sniper during a civil-rights march in Mississippi, my mother married Emory Garnell Smiley.

When I was three, the air force sent Garnell, my daddy, to Southeast Asia.

Mama had a newborn son, Emory—we called him Garnie. "The boys are going to miss you, Garnell," she told Dad.

"I'll be back before you know it. Don't you worry. Nothing's gonna get in the way of me getting back to my family," he promised.

At times I saw my mother crying during Dad's absence. Nothing—then or now—has upset me more. One time she began to cry when we were visiting a strange house. Mama and Big Mama, as I call my grandmother, were standing in front of a large wooden box that had been placed in the middle of the room. Mama and Big Mama were crying together.

"What's that box?" I asked a man in a dark suit.

"You call it a casket," he whispered in my ear.

"What's a casket?" I asked.

"Where they put dead people. Those who have gone home to the Lord."

"Who died?" I wanted to know.

"Your uncle Curtis. Your mother's brother."

Years later, I found out that my uncle had been living in Los

Angeles. His girlfriend had betrayed him for another man, and the other man had shot my uncle to death. The story gave me chills.

The best time to sit with my granddaddy, Paw Paw, was nighttime. The fireflies fluttered; somewhere in the distance an owl would hoot. Big Mama complained that Paw Paw was always drinking. I wasn't sure what drinking meant; all I knew was that I loved being with Paw Paw as he told me stories. I loved sitting in Paw Paw's lap on his rocking chair, rocking back and forth. His breath smelled sour and funny, but I didn't mind. He would puff on his corncob pipe and sip from his whiskey glass and speak in a honey-combed voice that was easy and slow.

"You see, son," he said one night, pointing his finger to the juke joint across the street, "over there is the bar room. You hear the women around here complaining about that bar room. They ain't wrong. I know I spend too much time up in there. But a man's got to have his peace of mind. A man's got to have his pleasure. Working down on the docks all day ain't no pleasure. It's good work, son, steady work, but it's sweat-and-blood work. You learn a lot about life on the docks. You'll see a lazy man who finds a way to get outta work; and you'll see a stand-up man who does the work he's paid to do. Well, I'm one of those stand-up men. But when the work is done and you're bone-tired, well, the bar room is a good place where men can go to wind down before going home to the ladies. There's fighting men in the bar room—you don't want nothing to do with them—but then you have your thinking men in the bar room. See, son, Paw Paw is a thinker. He's thinking about the life he's led and why your life is gonna be a whole lot better. He's thinking about how you've got a big, beautiful world in front of you. He's thinking that things are getting better all the time. And you're part of the better, Tavis. You're what's making this mean ol' world better."

And with that, he kissed me on the cheek, took another sip of whiskey, and went on rocking.


Not long afterward, I could see in Mama's face that she was worried.

"Death is frightening," she told Big Mama as they stood at the kitchen sink cleaning up the dishes from dinner. "The way Curtis was killed. The way Daddy's brother dropped dead out in the fields. Death just seems to come out of nowhere and swoop you up. And now Daddy's sick. I'm scared to death."

"We just gotta pray, baby," Big Mama told her. "We gotta pray night and day."

That night, I heard Paw Paw coughing so loudly it frightened me. I ran to my mother's room, where I overheard Mama's prayers. "Dear Lord," she said, "if my daddy dies, I'm giving my life to you. With all this death around me, I know I need you, Lord. I can't wait no longer. I need you in my life. I need to surrender my soul to you."

The next morning, Paw Paw was taken to the hospital.

"Will Paw Paw be home tonight?" I asked.

"No, baby," said Big Mama. "I know you love your Paw Paw, but Paw Paw is not feeling right. The doctors need to look after him."

"Will they have to put him in a casket?" I asked, tears rolling down my face.

"We pray not," Big Mama said, and hugged me. "We pray God will deliver him."

"It's his drinking," I heard my mother tell Big Mama. "All that drinking poisoned him."

At the end of the week, I found myself standing before another casket. My eyes were wet with tears as I watched it lowered into the ground. I heard my mother praying, "God, I am yours. I surrender my life to you."

Paw Paw was gone.


One day I heard Mama talking to a friend of hers around the kitchen table.

"My mama raised us up in the Baptist Church," said my mother.

"That's how I was raised up," said her friend. "That's the church I first knew."

"Remember how Mrs. Kelly joined the Church of God in Christ, and I told you all about it? Now Mrs. Kelly has been coming back around, talking to me."

"That's good. She's a God-fearing woman."

"She goes to the Holiness church now," said Mama.

"A lot of folk like that church."

"Mrs. Kelly says there's only one way to be saved. That makes sense to me, because with all these different denominations saving you in all these different ways, heaven would look just like this world. *Everyone* would be in heaven, and I know that's not right. I know there has to be just one way to be saved. Mrs. Kelly showed me the Scriptures that point to the way. They say the only way is to be baptized in the name of Jesus. Then God will speak through you. He'll speak through you in another language."

"That's when the Holy Ghost comes down," said her friend.

"That's when you speak in tongues. I know they speak in tongues at Elder Tate's Holiness church."

"Well, that's where I been going," Mama explained. "But I haven't been answering the altar call. Devil holds me back every time I start to walk down that aisle. Devil says, 'You can come back next week.' I try to resist, but I can't walk up that aisle. It's like the devil's holding me down. Like me and him are doing some serious hand-to-hand combat."

"If Elder Tate is speaking to your heart, your heart is hearing the truth. You gotta follow your heart, Joyce. You gotta go where the devil has no dominion. You gotta go to God."

On July 3, a Wednesday night, Mama and I were at Elder Tate's Holiness church, Apostolic Pentecostal. She had been tarrying all week. Tarrying, I would later learn, is a coaxing, prodding celebration of say-it-now, say-it-loud love of the Lord.

I was excited by the holy energy. The air was electric. A piano pounded out a rhythm that had the congregation jumping. I stepped into the aisle and began to do a little dance; the church folk urged me on. "Let him go. Let him get his praise on."

"Ain't he all right?" Elder Tate asked the congregation, whooping it up in the style of Reverend C. L. Franklin, Aretha's dad.

"Yes, he is," the congregation responded.

"I'm asking you, ain't he all right? Ain't he just all right?" Elder repeated.

"Oh, yes, he is!" everyone answered.

"Yes, he is!" I echoed in my little boy voice, happy to be part of the warmth of a congregation that loved the Lord with unrestrained passion.

"Now I know that tomorrow is the Fourth of July," said Elder

Tate. "That's a day when we party and eat barbecue and potato salad. Nothing wrong with barbecue. Nothing wrong with potato salad. But we got souls on this altar who have been tarrying for the Holy Ghost. And we're tarrying for them tonight. And I'm wondering if anyone will come back and tarry tomorrow."

The next day, the Fourth of July, Mama brought me back to church with my baby brother, Garnie.

Garnie sat on my lap, fast asleep. That he was able to sleep amazed me, because the women at the altar were praying in voices that could be heard across town. They were praying with all the power in their strong voices, tarrying for those who were awaiting the Holy Ghost.

The tarrying believers were up on their feet, waving their hands, repeating expressions of encouragement to my mother.

"Thank you, Jesus, thank you, Jesus . . ."

"Glory to God."

"Hallelujah! Hallelujah!"

"Jesus, Jesus, Jesus, Jesus, Jesus . . ."

"Praise him . . ."

"Praise him . . ."

"Praise him . . ."

The praises went on and on. But I wasn't bored, because there was music under the praise—a piano, an insistent drum beat, feet stomping, hands clapping. I could feel Mama's excitement. All the women in the church were excited as well, praising God and Jesus. The praise went on and on. Then, all at once Mama started shouting, and words flew out of her mouth that I couldn't understand.

"The Holy Ghost coming down! The Holy Ghost coming in!"

Tears streamed down Mama's face. She was crying, but they were happy tears. Her body shook as the Spirit of God washed over her like warm spring rain.

Before I could articulate it, I could feel it: the power of the church community to turn darkness to light, despair to hope, depression to joy. That little ol' rocking church in Gulfport, Mississippi, taught me a lesson that lives inside me today, that informs my spirit and lifts my heart when the world beats me down. The first church I attended, regardless of its doctrines, was the church that has kept me in church, in one form or another, for the rest of my life. Its connection to the black community, expressed in a music that set our souls soaring, has, as the song says, kept the circle unbroken.

"Your daddy is coming home," Mama told us ten months later, holding a letter from overseas. She told Big Mama and me that Daddy's tour of duty in Thailand and Taiwan had been completed. He'd be home in less than a month.

"Praise God!" Big Mama exclaimed.

"Praise God every day!" Mama reiterated. "Praise God in every way!"

# Gulfport to Bunker Hill

The land was flat as a pool table, and the cornfields went on forever. I could see cornfields from the windows of my school; we saw more cornfields when we rode to church on Sundays. I saw them in my dreams. To me, our new home in Indiana was one giant cornfield after another. And we were stuck right in the middle of it.

We had moved to Bunker Hill, Indiana, when Daddy had been restationed to Grissom Air Force Base, a few miles away. A small town, Bunker Hill had a population of 987. Main Street had only a single traffic light. From what I could tell, Bunker Hill was in the center of nowhere. The nearest larger towns were Kokomo and Peru, and they were small. Indianapolis, the state capital, lay 60 miles south. Chicago was 135 miles to the north, light-years away.

Bunker Hill was made up of farmers and the families of servicemen from Grissom Air Force Base. There were only a couple of black families in town. We now lived in a landlocked white world of yellow cornfields, in a crowded trailer inside a trailer park.

———

Nothing could keep Mama from putting church in the center of our lives. We started searching for the right church our first Sunday morning in town.

"It has to be a *righteous* church," Mama told Daddy.

Mama was in charge of the search, and she handled our search the way she took charge of the family finances. Believe me, Mama could stretch a dollar; she was the best money manager in the county. Daddy liked how Mama was determined to keep our family strong and connected by anchoring us to a church that offered true salvation.

Mama was wearing a beautiful green dress that matched her eyes. Dad was handsomely dressed in his tailored blue suit. And I was dressed like a royal prince—blue jacket, white shirt, red tie, shiny black shoes, and a cool hat to match.

We rode alongside the cornfields on our way to Peru to visit churches. When we arrived, Peru was practically deserted. Dad drove around until he found a medium-sized church.

"That's it," said Mama. "That's the church I was told about."

We got out of the car. Mama walked quickly and with purpose. We heard an organ playing from inside the sanctuary. We looked inside through a window and saw that the church was filled with white people.

"Don't matter," said Mama. "We're all God's children. Let's go in."

But when Daddy tried to open the door, he found it locked.

"That's wrong," Mama said. "Why would they lock the door to a church?"

So Mama decided to drive to Kokomo instead. "Kokomo's a bigger town."

We drove twenty miles to Kokomo, where Mama spotted a black man walking down Jefferson Street. She told Dad to pull over.

"Good morning, sir," said Mama. "Can you tell us if there's a Holiness church around here?"

"Well, Brother Green preaches at a church on Monroe Street. And then there's Elder Rufus Mills over there on Elm Street."

"Thank you, sir," said Mama, declaring, "Thank you, Jesus!" as we drove down the street. The key for her was "Elder," the title the Holiness church gives its preachers.

A few minutes later we were walking up the stairs of the New Bethel Tabernacle Church at 704 East Elm Street. We found an empty pew near the front. As we sat down, an elderly woman turned to Mama and asked, "You been saved?"

"Yes, ma'am."

"You got the Holy Ghost?"

"Yes, ma'am."

"That's good. You been baptized in the name of Jesus?"

"Yes, ma'am."

"Glory!" exclaimed the lady. "Glory be to God!"

And so we were welcomed into the church.

On the way back to Bunker Hill, Mama recounted all that we had to be thankful for.

"Look at the God we serve," she said. "Brought us all the way from Gulfport to Indiana. Locked the doors to a church that wasn't the right church anyway. Then brought us to Kokomo and let that man say 'Elder.' Took us right to the church where they baptize in Jesus' name, where they got the Holy Ghost, and where they speak in tongues. Who says the Lord isn't protecting this family? Who says God isn't good?"

# The Trailer and the Church

In 1970, if you drove up Highway U.S. 31 a ways, you'd see a big banner that said "Trailers for Sale." A dozen brand-new trailer homes were parked in the sales lot. Beyond the new units stood several rows of forty or fifty older trailers, where families rented.

Our own trailer was green and white. We had two small bedrooms in the back and a bedroom for Mama and Daddy up front. The trailer park was adjacent to a large field where we played baseball all hours of the day. Daddy could be at work in just a couple of minutes, as Grissom Air Force Base was right across Highway 31.

When I asked Daddy why we couldn't live in a regular house, he said, "You see, son, I'm only an E-4, which means I have three stripes. I'm low on the totem pole. That's why we can't get housing on the base. There's hardly any rental housing in the local community. But trailers are plentiful and they are economical. Your mother will tell you that economy is the key. We have to live within our means."

My daddy was a strong man who exuded confidence and integrity. I loved how when he dressed in his air-force blues, he would top off the uniform by wearing his long narrow hat cocked slightly to the side. I loved to watch him shine and buff his shoes. I was amazed at the care he showed as he worked the black leather into a mirror finish. I could sit and watch him shine his shoes for hours. I also loved his walk. He had a little dip in his gait that everyone thought was cool. Daddy had his own style of stepping. Later, I'd learn that the dip wasn't the result of his desire to look cool; he was born with polio and one leg was shorter than the other.

Daddy was as dark-skinned as Mama was light, as soft-spoken as Mama was boisterous. He was as easygoing as Mom was serious. Dad made the money. Mom ran the household. Each complemented the other. But they both loved to laugh, and their laughter was infectious. They formed a united front that couldn't be broken.

I loved and trusted my daddy. He liked to quote Popeye: "I am what I am and that's all I am." There were no pretenses about him, no sense of his wanting to be something he wasn't. He was a worker, up at the crack of dawn. And his devotion to our family was heroic.

It was Mama who got Daddy hooked into the Holiness church in Kokomo. Dad saw the value in attending church regularly and went along with Mama's program.

"Church will give this family a focus, Tabo"—his nickname for me—"and a focus on values and discipline will keep all of you out of trouble."

Dad got the Holy Ghost during a Sunday service at the New Bethel Tabernacle Church. There was great rejoicing. Dad was waving his arms in celebration, Mama was weeping, and everyone rejoiced. I couldn't help but be happy. I started jumping around like I used to in the church back in Gulfport. In the Kokomo church, though, folks looked at me funny when I "got my praise on." They, too, praised God, but they did so with more restraint. I wanted to shout and holler. I wanted to run up and down the aisles with the good feeling that God put in my feet. I wanted to let my spirit run free. But that clearly wasn't this church's way.

When Elder Mills heard I could sing, he put me in the children's choir. I loved being in the choir, and I sang my heart out. If I couldn't all-out dance to express my joy in the Lord, at least I could sing that joy. One way or another, I had to let the good feeling flow out of me.

Soon, we drove back to church every evening for one activity or another. Mama and Dad became church leaders. In the white world of rural Indiana, our black church was our spiritual home, our rock. And our family's belief never wavered. Among the hundred or so members of the New Bethel Tabernacle Church, Joyce Marie Roberts Smiley and Emory Garnell Smiley quickly became regarded as pillars, winning the respect of the entire congregation.

Mama was the disciplinarian in our family, and she definitely did not spare the rod. Mama's anger was something to behold. When my mother was happy, all was well with the world. She laughed and talked at the top of her voice. But when she was paying the family bills, you learned to leave her alone. Mama was an enthusiast who wore her heart on her sleeve. She told you just what she was feeling; she was incapable of holding back. Whatever she did, she did with great passion.

Her quick temper, though, could be frightening. Lord knows it frightened my siblings and me. Unlike Dad, whose temperament was cool, Mama's temperament ran hot. She didn't hesitate to smack us when she felt it necessary. At the time, I couldn't understand. When Mom got to whipping us, the expression I hated most was, "This hurts me more than it hurts you." *Baloney*, I thought to myself. *If that's the case, you wouldn't be doing no whipping.*

Only a lifetime later could I understand that, with a trailer filled with children, my parents had to maintain order. Mama's job was to do just that. To lose that sense of order, she believed, was to lose control of her kids. For us to maintain a decent lifestyle outside the trailer, we had to develop a sense of decent behavior inside the trailer. That was Mama's philosophy of child rearing, and no one ever questioned it.

"It was never this cold in Mississippi," Mama complained one Saturday morning in January.

It was our first winter in Indiana, and the walls of the trailer weren't thick enough to insulate us from the near-zero temperature outside. The heat was on full blast but it wasn't nearly enough. Only the gospel music booming out of the stereo—the Edwin Hawkins Singers singing "Oh, Happy Day"—seemed to warm us up a little. We played the song over and over again. I wanted to watch Saturday-morning cartoons or listen to the Jackson Five on the radio—someone told me that the Jacksons were from Indiana—but Mama wouldn't allow it. She wouldn't allow us to go to the movies, either. The New Bethel Tabernacle Church frowned on movies.

That morning, the phone rang. Mama answered the phone cheerily, as she always did, but this time her cheerfulness didn't last long. Her face collapsed into a terrible grimace. She dropped the phone, crying out, "Garnell! Garnell! I need you right now!"

Dad was outside. I ran out there to get him.

"My sister's dead," Mama cried out as he rushed to her side. "My sister's been murdered."

"My God," said Dad, holding Mama. "What happened?"

"That bar room across the street from our house in Gulfport— that bar room where Daddy used to drink?"

"Yes?"

"She went in there looking for her boyfriend. They argued. When she turned her back on him, he pulled a gun on her and shot her. Shot her in cold blood, in the back. Killed my sister, Garnell . . ."

Mama was crying so hard the words stuck in her throat. "She has all those children," said Daddy.

"And now," said Mama, her face streaked with tears, "those children have no mother."

We rode the Greyhound down to Gulfport for the funeral. It was the saddest ride I have ever experienced. For the most part, Mama just sat there, her eyes filled with tears. Sometimes she'd tell me the stories about her sister and the life they shared as children. Sometimes she'd talk about her sister's kids. She was praying for them, she told me. She was praying that out of this situation these kids could be saved. Mama was praying so hard I could feel her prayers washing all over me. "Help my family," she prayed. "Help us all."

# Men Were Walking on the Moon

The assassination of RFK, the assassination of Martin Luther King, the assassination of Malcolm X—these tragedies passed over me like fast-moving clouds. It was all above my head. For many years after, the news from around the world blew through our family like a brief storm, leaving no remnant of its passing. The Israeli athletes killed at the Olympics in 1972, the Paris Peace talks and the Vietnam peace pact in 1973, Watergate and President Nixon's resignation.

Our home in Bunker Hill was centered on work and God, rather than national news. With one great exception, the secular world was largely ignored, or kept firmly at bay. That exception was Muhammad Ali.

"He's the man!" my dad would declare. "I like how he conducts himself both in and out of the ring. But especially *in* the ring."

Sitting next to Dad, listening to our floor-model Philco TV, I watched Ali mow down a slew of heavyweight opponents over the years—Jerry Quarry, Floyd Patterson, Ken Norton, Joe Frazier—all to our delight.

As a kid, I had few father-son moments. Watching Muhammad Ali with Dad was one of the rare ones. My father was always working, so sitting next to him watching TV was a particular pleasure. He liked *The Rockford Files* and *Charlie's Angels,* but he *loved* Muhammad Ali.

I loved Ali not only because Dad loved him, but because Ali was a brilliant athlete who used his brain as much as his brawn. I also loved him for his verbal agility. He could not only outpunch his opponent, he could talk rings around him. Ali was a poet and prankster. He was hyperarticulate and surely the most confident man in America. The fact that a black man projected such self-respect while displaying disregard for the opinion of the white media endeared him to us even more. You just had to respect him. He was our champ. I paid far more attention to the major events in Ali's career than to the global events reported on the evening news.

But if great world events did not seem to impact our household, personal events did. And nothing changed the Smiley family more than the death of my mother's sister.

For a while, Big Mama, who continued to live in Gulfport, cared for my aunt's five children. But Big Mama was growing older, and the job of chasing after five young kids sapped her energy. She desperately needed help.

One morning, Mama and Daddy discussed the situation before Daddy went off to work.

"Joyce," Dad said to Mama, "the right thing to do is to take these children in as our own. I saw my parents do it with my sisters. I feel like it's something we should do."

"The burden on Big Mama is getting to be too much," Mama agreed.

"That's what I'm saying, baby. The responsibility has to fall on us. And we have to accept it."

"And you don't mind, Garnell?"

"I'll find extra work. We'll find a way to manage. It'll work out."

"God has led me to a good man in you, Garnell," said Mama.

In the summer of 1974, my cousins arrived from Gulfport, Mississippi.

"They are not your cousins," Dad reprimanded me when I talked about my cousins' imminent arrival. "From now on, they are your sisters and brothers."

And so it was, from that day on, I had two new sisters and two new brothers—Pam, Phyllis, Paul, and Patrick. (A third girl stayed in Gulfport.) Nor was I the oldest child any longer. My new sisters were both older than me—Pam was two years older, and Phyllis was a year older. And Mama gave birth to two more sons in the years that followed. In addition to my little brothers Garnie, Maury, and Derwin (whom we call Dubby), Mama gave birth to Weldon (whom we call Scooter) and Trenton Dion.

Eventually, Big Mama left Mississippi and came to live with us in Indiana. In a few years, our family had grown to thirteen.

Although we remained in a trailer park, we did move up to a double-wide trailer. Nonetheless, thirteen people in a trailer, double-wide or not, made for close quarters.

Dad responded to our increased financial need in his typically heroic fashion—he started a second job and soon put the Smiley kids to work, as well. You can imagine the waiting lines in front of the bathroom.

And Mama responded in her typical fashion—managing the money even more closely and supervising the household chores, while making sure all of us doubled our devotion to church.

Our family became a highly disciplined, highly regimented crew. Any other approach likely would have led to chaos.

Mama was the enforcer. If we got out of line, we were sent off to find a switch. And Mom brandished the switch with gusto, whether pregnant or not. "You will not get out of line again," she would repeat over and over again as one of us felt the harsh sting of her anger.

It was Mom who set up our daily schedule at church, to ensure that our souls received as much attention and nourishment as our minds. A typical week in our lives at the church looked like this:

Monday, 7 P.M.: prayer meeting

Tuesday, 7 P.M.: choir rehearsal

Wednesday, 7 P.M.: Bible class

Thursday, 7 P.M.: missionary meeting

Friday, 7 P.M.: young people's meeting

Saturday, 9 A.M.: prayer meeting

Saturday, 10 A.M.: Emory Smiley and his kids clean the church for Sunday services

Saturday, 11 A.M.: Junior Choir rehearsal

Sunday, 9:45 A.M.: Sunday school

Sunday, 11:30 A.M.: morning worship

Sunday, 5:30 P.M.: children's church

Sunday, 7 P.M.: evening service

We followed this schedule for most of my years growing up in Indiana. In many ways, in different arenas, I continue to follow the course set by my Mama to this day.

But my Daddy, too, had an enormous influence on my life. When I turned ten, my Daddy suggested setting up a family cleaning business called Smiley & Sons. I first learned of his plan when I overheard him excitedly explain the idea to Mama.

"The air-force base awards contracts to cleaning companies," he said. "And those companies do a mediocre job. Well, I've talked to my superiors and convinced them that if I supervise a cleaning crew, the work will be done right. All sorts of buildings on the base need to be cleaned nightly. Our kids are old enough to help, and each job represents extra cash in our pockets. What do you think, Joyce?"

"I think you're a wonderful provider, Garnell, that's what I think."

And so Smiley & Sons was born, without so much as a conversation with Daddy's "employees." Every day we got home from school at 2:30 P.M. and did our homework. Every night after church, my sisters and brothers and I changed into work clothes and headed out to the base. On Mondays we cleaned the credit union. Tuesdays, we cleaned the barracks. Wednesdays, we cleaned the pediatrician's office. We cleaned the post office on Thursdays and the dental office on Fridays. Dad walked alongside us, helping us mop, scrub, dust, wax, wash windows, and empty trash.

Home by ten, we were asleep in no time.

Later in life, someone asked me what I learned from being one of ten kids living in a trailer. My quick answer was that I learned I never wanted to live in a trailer again. I never wanted to be poor again. I saw the small amount of money my dad made in the military and, right then and there, decided that a military life was not for me. I would go elsewhere—I would go to college.

On the other hand, I learned the value of family. Mama illustrated the great gift of sharing on our birthdays. Because there was no money to spare, there were no presents to buy. Instead, on your birthday Mama baked you your favorite cake or pie. You had the honor of cutting it up and presenting a slice to each of your siblings. What remained was yours. As a result, your generosity was on display for all to see. Your greed, demonstrated by slicing extra-thin slivers, would be greeted with groans from your brothers and sisters. Your willingness to share, demonstrated by good-sized portions, would be greeted with cheers. Our sharing was rewarded with others' goodwill, a lesson that couldn't be ignored.

When our family ballooned to thirteen members, even the double-wide trailer barely contained us. Mama and Daddy had a bedroom in the back. Garnie and I slept in bunk beds up front. My two sisters and Big Mama shared the second back bedroom. The others slept on a pullout sofa bed in the living room. From time to time, the configuration changed. I spent a great deal of my childhood being peed upon by one of my brothers in the middle of the night. My brothers would torture each other by drinking huge quantities of water at bedtime. The results were preordained. With eight boys in the trailer, the energy and testosterone were tough to contain.

That same energy, though, found a more productive outlet on the field adjacent to the trailer park. This ball field was a piece of heaven for young kids cooped up during the winter months.

After the March winds died down and the April showers turned everything green, the field came alive. We would work all week in school and church, and at night, as Smiley & Sons, we'd clean up the base. Our reward was Saturday-afternoon baseball. I was a good first baseman and a Cincinnati Reds fanatic. This was during the seventies, the heyday of the Big Red Machine when manager Sparky Anderson and Johnny Bench, Pete Rose, Joe Morgan, Tony Perez, and Ken Griffey Sr. were helping the club win championships. I dreamed of joining the Reds. In part my hopes were based on our own success in Little League. The Smiley brothers were the best in the area. As a family, we were large enough to field a team of our own. And as brothers, we anticipated each other's moves. We had absorbed Dad's discipline practicing together and played like pros. It felt great to be the best at something, a feeling I wanted to experience and taste again and again. To some degree, it even made up for being peed on at night. Garnie was a powerhouse pitcher who gave the opposition fits. Living in rural Indiana, we were about the only black players around, which gave us another reward. Beating the white boys felt particularly good.

I looked out the window from my sixth-grade classroom and watched the rains wash over the cornfields. The wind blew so strongly I wondered if the stalks would break as they swayed and bent.

"You seem very far away, Tavis," said Mrs. Vera Graft, my grade school teacher. "You look like you're daydreaming again."

Mama had already been to school to speak to Mrs. Graft. The only time Mom missed church, in fact, was for a teacher's conference. She'd informed me that Mrs. Graft wasn't happy with my performance or attitude. I just wasn't motivated. The only way I'd learned my multiplication was by Mom cracking my knuckles at night.

I'd had a hard time adjusting to school in Indiana. In Mississippi, my classmates were all black. My preschool teacher, Mrs. Warren, a black woman who brought out the best in her students, had encouraged me.

Here, though, all my classmates and teachers were white. As the only black student in the class, I felt like an outsider.

After class, Mrs. Graft came over to my desk.

"You have a bright and alert mind," Mrs. Graft told me sternly, but like Mama, with a caring tone. "You're gifted with a fine intelligence, Tavis. But you have to apply it. When we read, you act like you're not interested. When we do arithmetic, you act like you don't care. I don't think you're trying hard enough."

I couldn't look Mrs. Graft in the eye. I knew she was right. Glancing out the window, I could see a rainbow arched over the sky from one end of the world to the other.

"When you look at that magnificent rainbow, Tavis," she said, following my gaze, "think of the beauty that lies ahead of you. Your life will be full of beauty, because you're a beautiful person. You can achieve whatever you want to achieve. You can follow that rainbow—do wonderful things, meet wonderful people, see wonderful places. There are no limits on what you can do. You're different from the others in this class, Tavis. The color of your skin is different. But listen to me when I say that you are just as smart, if not smarter, and just as good as anyone here. And I mean *anyone*. It's time to quit quitting, Tavis. Deep down, I know you're not a quitter. You're an achiever. And if you work at it, you're going to get that pot at the end of the rainbow."

As I did my homework that night, Mrs. Graft's words echoed inside me. As I attended choir rehearsal, as I helped Smiley & Sons clean up barracks on the base, her words replayed in my mind: *Time to quit quitting*.

That night I dreamed of rainbows—thousands of Technicolor rainbows illuminating fields of gold.

*You can achieve your heart's desire.*

*You can get that pot at the end of the rainbow.*

I knew Mrs. Graft was right.

Looking back, I now understand that not all kids are motivated to achieve. I wasn't. I needed encouragement. I needed some-one to take special interest in me. It was significant that, for a black child in an overwhelmingly white environment, that interest came from a white teacher. Mrs. Graft was telling me that I was as good as anyone, white or black. She showed me that a single mentor, especially early on, can transform your attitude about yourself. On the deepest level, she was showing me love.

I was seeing in grade school—as I'd continue to see in high school—the undeniable fact that people of all races can get along. Throughout my childhood, this was not theory but demonstrable truth. I saw it before my very eyes. I lived it. The peculiar situation I found myself in—growing up in a rural state with a racist history—proved to be a blessing. I was able to see that people are capable of change. I got to affirm what I later found to be a cornerstone of the great American civil-rights movement—that, no matter how dire the circumstances, we can overcome.

# The Bully and the Lesson

My daddy was a tremendously hard worker. Work dominated his life. He considered his obligation—to provide for ten kids, a wife, and a mother-in-law—a holy mandate. He took on the task without complaints or regrets. He just did it. In that regard, he was heroic. At times, though, in dealing with us he could be heavy-handed.

I remember one Saturday when he was outside working on a neighbor's car. Dad was an expert mechanic who, in addition to his regular job in the military and after-hours work with Smiley & Sons, repaired cars. That's what he was doing on this freezing February morning. After a half hour of working alone, he came inside to recruit me.

"I want you out here, Tabo," he ordered. "I want you to help me."

"I can't, Dad," I explained. "I have too much homework."

"The homework can wait," he said. "The car can't. Besides, I want to show you some things about this engine."

There was nothing about the engine I wanted to see, nothing about cars I wanted to know. I didn't care about cars—not then, not now. At age forty-one, I still have never bought a new car.

"Dad," I complained, "I just can't."

"You can't or you won't?"

"It's freezing cold out there, Dad, and I wouldn't be any help anyway."

"I'm tired of arguing with you."

"You know I'm no good with cars."

"Well, it's time you learned."

"I don't want to learn."

"Great," my dad shot back, "you'll grow up to be a faggot."

"Faggot" was the ultimate insult my dad could hurl. He was undoubtedly homophobic. He wouldn't call it that, though. Since the church insisted all homosexuals are going to hell, he'd call his view of homosexuality scripturally sound. So in calling me a faggot, he was telling me that I was going to hell, that I was less than a man, that because I had no interest in cars, I would wind up a sissy.

His words stung. I had no answer for him. And I had no way of telling him how deeply the accusation wounded me. I was devastated.

"Your daddy has to work hard," said Big Mama, who had overheard the exchange, "because money is so tight. Sometimes when men work hard they say things they don't mean."

Only when I became an adult did I begin to understand the precarious position my father was in. He was a Southerner in the Midwest, a black man fighting poverty in a white world, a military professional for whom no-nonsense discipline was a way of life. As a kid, I couldn't imagine the emotional pressures on him, the daily battle for dignity, the unrelenting struggle for survival.

Money *was* tight in the Smiley household, especially after we adopted my cousins. We had no family doctor or dentist. Fortunately, I was never sick, nor it seemed, were my brothers and sisters. It was just as well because we had no money for medical care. When someone suggested to Mama that our family was blessed with good luck, she replied, "It isn't good luck. It's blessing from a good God."

Mama held a tight rein on the finances. I didn't have new shoes every year. My old shoes might have had a hole in the sole, but they'd have to do. Same was true for last year's blue jeans. If they were short, they were short. If they looked uncool, too bad.

When Pam, Phyllis, Paul, and Patrick arrived, part of me was disappointed that I was no longer the eldest child. Part of me was resentful that our space was being invaded and our money, already stretched thin, was being stretched even thinner. I knew it would mean less of everything for me. Kids tend to think of themselves first, and I was a kid.

As I moved from elementary to middle school, my classmates continued to be almost all white. The black families who were transferred to Grissom Air Force Base didn't stay long. They found ways of switching to urban areas with larger black populations. Most of the white folks who were not in the air force worked in agriculture and earned very little. Even the steel plants in Kokomo were closing down.

More poor white people had moved into our already-crowded trailer park. Kids in school would refer to them as "trailer-park trash." *But if they were trash,* I wondered, *what did that make us?* The poor whites moving in had more than we did—bigger trailers, bigger TV sets, more clothes for their kids. If poverty has different levels—as it surely does—we were at the bottom.

By seventh grade, I'd developed into a prodigious talker.

Words came easily to me. Ever since I'd started school, I'd been extremely verbal. In fact, back in Mrs. Graft's second-grade class I was already getting into trouble for talking too much. By fourth grade I was writing plays and skits. Not long after that I was reading Scripture in front of the entire church. I saw words as friends. I liked how they sounded slipping off my tongue. They made me feel powerful. I quickly gained a reputation as a motormouth.

In the beginning I was arrogant about my ability with words. I'd use my verbal skills to put others down. I was articulate, and if you weren't, I might rub it in your face. And I could be merciless. Every week I'd learn the list of new words provided by *Reader's Digest* and employ them in speech or sentences. I was far ahead of the curve, throwing around words like *paradoxical* and *antithetical* that most of my classmates didn't understand.

Mama saw what was happening. Mama saw everything that was going on with her children. But how was she to correct this especially egregious character fault, especially when it was born out of my drive to achieve?

The answer came with a little souvenir. Mama and Daddy had just returned from a weekend they had spent in Brown County in southern Indiana. It was their only vacation away from us that I can remember.

"Brought you something," said Mama soon after they got back.

She handed me a little wooden pencil holder with words written on the side: "It's hard to be humble when you're as great as I am."

"Do you know why I bought this for you, Tavis?" she asked.

"Because I'm great."

"Well, you are great, but that's not why I bought it."

"Because I need to be humble and I'm not."

"That's more like it, Tavis."

"I guess I don't exactly see why I should be humble when I know I'm good at something."

"When you get to feeling like that," she said, "look at this pencil holder and read those words out loud. Sooner or later their wisdom will sink in. Look, Tavis, you're a bright boy and I thank the Lord for your intelligence. You don't ever have to apologize for that intelligence. What you put in your head no one—not even the white man—can take away. But there's a problem, Tavis, when you stick that intelligence in people's faces. People don't like that, and they don't like you for doing it. In praising yourself, you're making them feel bad. The trick, Tavis, is to let others praise you. That praise will come, and it will come naturally. So next time you do something great, next time you say something clever, I don't want you to tell anyone. I want you to watch and see if a compliment doesn't come your way without your prompting it. When that compliment does arrive, it'll be that much sweeter, knowing it was given freely and sincerely."

The next day at school, when I recited the entire lineup of the Cincinnati Reds, along with each player's current batting averages, I didn't say a word or challenge my classmate to do the same. After a few seconds, my classmate just looked at me and said, "Wow, Tavis, that's amazing. How do you remember all that?"

Mama was right.

Mama was probably right about another difficult area of behavior. That area, though, involved more than talking; it had to do with physical fighting.

Ralph was a big high school kid with a reputation as a bully. One day he was sitting across from me on the bus. (Both middle and high school kids took the same bus.) He also happened to live in our trailer park. Ralph and his friend were talking baseball. Ralph was telling the other kid that last year Pete Rose had had the highest slugging percentage on the Reds.

"That's not true," I broke in.

"Who's talking to you, Smiley?" Ralph challenged me.

"I know the slugging percentages," I said. "Morgan, Bench, Perez, and even Dan Driessen had better percentages than Rose."

"You don't know nothing," Ralph shot back.

"In fact," I retorted, "I'm sure that Rose has never led the team in slugging percentage during any season—"

"Butt out."

"Okay, if you're not interested in the facts . . ." I said, matter-of-factly.

"Do you know what I'm interested in?" Ralph asked.

"No," I answered.

"I'm interested in beating your butt. You interested in getting your butt beat, Smiley?"

"No."

"Well, you better get interested, 'cause the minute we get off this bus I'm coming after you."

"Why?"

"Because you're a punk and I like beating up punks."

Ralph wasn't kidding; in fact, he was dead serious. For the final ten minutes of the bus ride, my palms sweated and my heart raced. My sisters Pam and Phyllis were with me, and they heard the whole thing. Pam and Phyllis were strong and gutsy, and their natural instinct was to come to my defense. But they were wearing dresses. Mom demanded that they wear dresses every day of the year. Back then, girls in dresses couldn't even think about fighting. I was on my own.

The bus doors opened. As I got off, I felt Ralph's breath on my neck. The minute the doors closed and the bus pulled away, he started punching me with all his might. Rather than fight back, I covered my face with my hands, fell to my knees, and absorbed his punches.

"This is what you're gonna get every day, Smiley. Every day I see you on this bus, I'm beating your butt."

And with that, he walked into his trailer. Only a few yards away, at our trailer, my brothers were watching. They'd seen everything.

I went inside and said nothing to Mama.

Next day, when Pam, Phyllis, and I rode the bus to school, Ralph reminded me that at the end of the day he was going to beat me up.

At the end of the day he did just that. I assumed the position and he took his swings. My brothers and sisters watched; I was completely humiliated. When I thought about my hero Muhammad Ali, my humiliation only deepened.

Ralph continued beating me for weeks. School became torture to me. I couldn't get my mind off the beating that awaited me at the end of the day.

"Why don't you fight back?" my siblings asked me.

The fact was that I was too scared. I was afraid he'd beat me even more. I was only in seventh grade, while he was in high school.

Somewhere along the line Mama heard about these beatings. As I descended from the bus on the Monday of the third week, I caught a glimpse of her standing in front of our trailer, watching what was becoming a painful ritual.

After Ralph knocked me around, I picked up my books and walked to the trailer. Mama asked me, "How long has this been going on?"

"Awhile," I answered.

"Go to your room, Tavis."

Whenever my mom said, "Go to your room," that meant we were getting a beating.

Our beatings came frequently, but never for cursing or cutting school. None of us would dare do that. And the idea of talking back to our parents wasn't even a consideration. Nor was drinking or smoking. We'd get whupped for bad grades and misbehaving in school. If any cookie jar money was missing—even a dime—Mama would line us all up and beat every one of us until someone confessed.

This time, however, I wasn't sure that Mama was going to give me a beating. For a moment I prayed that she would call Ralph's parents and angrily insist that he stop. But Mama had other ideas. Without another word, Mama came into the room, took a belt and beat the daylights out of me. In fact, far from meting out sympathy, Mama beat me far worse than Ralph did.

"Every day that you let Ralph beat you," she said, "you're gonna get another beating from me. You cannot let people disrespect you. You need to learn to defend yourself."

I wasn't happy with Mama's reaction. It seemed excessive to me. Wasn't one beating enough? But I understood what she meant. She didn't see any other way to get me to defend myself. She knew extreme measures were necessary.

At first Mama's ultimatum did not change things. Every day I got off the bus and got beat up by Ralph. Then I went into our trailer and was beaten by Mama. When Ralph learned about my mother's beatings, he tortured me even more. "Your own mama is whupping you," he said. "You're a punk. Everyone thinks you're a punk."

Then one Friday, everything changed.

The sky was pearl gray, the ground icy. I could see my breath in the air. My winter jacket was torn and too thin to protect me from the cold. My wool cap was dotted with moth holes. I was miserable. I had had enough. As I stepped off the bus, Ralph, as always, stepped off behind me. I felt him breathing down my neck. I waited for the sting of his first punch. I could see my mother standing in front of our trailer, a belt in her hand. But as I started to assume the position, something in me snapped. I looked Ralph in the eye and, just like that, hauled off and punched him square in the mouth. The punch was solid and surprisingly strong. It was so strong, in fact, that Ralph went down. As he started to get up, I went after him. This time, despite the dresses they were wearing, Pam and Phyllis went after him as well. I fought so fiercely that I broke Ralph's arm. In the mayhem, Pam broke her collarbone. But in the eyes of Mama and my brothers, I was redeemed. And from then on, Ralph left me alone.

Mama's lesson came through loud and clear and stayed with me for the rest of my life.

You must stand up for yourself.

You must face your fears.

You must defeat those fears by moving straight ahead.

Big Mama had a lesson of her own for me.

In the back of our trailer, she was alone in the room she shared with my sisters, praying loudly. I loved when Big Mama prayed out loud. You could hear her big, boisterous voice halfway around the world.

"Thank you, Jesus," she prayed. "Thank you, Lord. Thank you for another day. Thank you for my children. Thank you for my children's children. Thank you for my health, Lord. Thank you for letting me walk and talk and see and breathe. Thank you for letting me feel you, Lord. Thank you for setting me free."

She looked up and saw me standing in the doorway.

"Tavis," she said, "I heard all about your blessing."

"Blessing, Big Mama?"

"You and that bully."

"How is that a blessing?"

"There's a lesson and a blessing in everything we go through."

"Okay, what's the lesson, and what's the blessing?"

"The lesson is that you don't need to be afraid. And the blessing is that your family, even your sisters, shared in the battle. We're blessed to be in a family where we share each other's good times and bad."

"But, Big Mama, it took me such a long time to stand up to Ralph."

"Takes as long as it takes. When folk in church get impatient to hear from God, the saints say, 'He may not be there when you want him, but the Lord's always right on time.' You were right on time, Tavis. Your change came right on time."

And with that, Big Mama broke into one of her famous, uproarious, warm, infectious laughs. I started laughing too, until my sides ached, until the pain and confusion surrounding my daily beatings by Ralph dissolved like a bad dream.

There would be plenty of other times in my life when I would have to stand up to bullies and those who wanted to bring me down. But I never forgot my experience with Ralph. It was far better to confront those who oppressed me head-on, I realized, than allow them to demean and disrespect me.

# The Revelation

My father was alone in one of the Grissom Air Force Base airplane hangars. The hangar was enormous. The planes housed inside, immaculate and poised for flight, intimidated me. I watched my dad climb over and under each plane, using his arsenal of tools to calibrate the complex engines.

I was in awe of Dad not only because of his technical expertise but because of the devotion he showered on us. He was one man supporting thirteen. Aside from bringing in the money, working fourteen-hour days, he was as conscientious a churchgoer as Mom. At New Bethel Tabernacle, the Smiley family owned the second pew. Virtually every Sunday and every night of the week, we marched in like an army of loyal soldiers, committed to serving God.

Dad spotted me in the back of the hangar watching him. He smiled and motioned to me to come to his side. I ran over and he started to explain the details of the engines he was repairing. The information went over my head, but that didn't matter. I was proud of him, proud to be his son. He was a man of intelligence and responsibility whom the air force had trusted with duties of the gravest importance, maintaining the engines that allowed planes to fly.

On the way home, in our old station wagon, Dad talked more about his hero, Muhammad Ali. Dad never tired of analyzing Ali's moves. That Saturday afternoon, Mom and Dad went grocery shopping. My chores were done, and I wanted to sneak in a little TV.

While we could watch certain family shows like *Gilligan's Island, Love Boat*, and *Flip Wilson,* we were not allowed to see *Roots,* which my parents thought contained too much nudity. The movie theaters were off limits as well. We never saw *Shaft* or *Superfly* or any of the popular blaxploitation films. We didn't own a single record by Barry White or Al Green, Sly Stone or George Clinton. Other than gospel, the music I knew best was the stuff the white kids listened to on their radios at school—rock 'n' roll from groups like AC/DC, Pink Floyd, and Supertramp.

Despite Mom's dictum prohibiting secular music in the trailer, there were times when I cheated. This was one of those times. The Jackson Five were slated to be on *Soul Train.* There was no way I could miss them. Their new hit, "Dancing Machine," with its intoxicating rhythms, was one of my favorites. In fact, Michael Jackson was my idol. In truth, I dreamed of renaming myself Michael and losing Tavis, a name I had always disliked.

I turned on the TV to *Soul Train.* Just as the Jackson Five were kicking off their amazing dance routine, my sister Pam interrupted me.

"You watched *Soul Train* last week," she said. "I wanna watch *Bionic Woman.*"

"Oh, come on, Pam," I said, "I'm watching the Jackson Five. *Bionic Woman* is silly."

"If you don't turn it off, I'm telling your mom."

"You tell Mama about the *Soul Train,* and I'm telling her how you watch *Bionic Woman.*"

"I've seen your daddy watching *Bionic Woman.*"

"No, you haven't," I said. "He wouldn't watch that show."

"You think you know him, but you don't. You don't even know that he's not even your real daddy."

That stopped me cold. A terrible fear opened within me. "What are you talking about?"

"Garnell Smiley is not your father. You don't even know who your real father is."

"He is so my father. You're making this up, Pam."

"I'm telling the truth, Tavis. Just ask your mom," she smirked.

When Mama came home, I asked her if what Pam had said was true. Was Garnell Smiley my real father? Hearing my question, Mama's face seemed to crumble. She began to cry uncontrollably. And suddenly my heart was breaking. I knew that Pam had told the truth.

"Your father is T," she said between tears. "I've kept this from you because I didn't want to hurt you. I didn't want you to think that Garnell isn't your dad, because he *is* your dad. Not your biological dad, but your true dad, the dad who took you in as his own when he married me, who loved you and raised you as his own son. I wanted to wait till you were older and more mature. I'm sorry." Mama continued crying. "I wanted to be the one to tell you. I didn't want you to learn this way."

Mama's news stunned me. I didn't know what to think. Every assumption I had about my upbringing, my family, and my life was torn asunder. For years I wondered why my younger brother Garnie had been given my father's first name and I hadn't. Now I knew. I'd been teased by boys at school for having a name like Tavis, but I never really questioned how I got it.

I walked to the back of the trailer. Big Mama was sitting up in bed, reading her Bible. She motioned for me to sit beside her. On her lap was a quilt she was sewing, a series of multicolored circles and squares.

"I heard all that crying," she said.

"You knew the truth, didn't you?" I asked.

"Sure I knew. And you would have learned the truth in due time. But learning it now just brings on the lesson and the blessing that much quicker."

"I don't get the lesson, Big Mama, and I don't feel the blessing."

"Look here, Tavis. The lesson is that a man can be your real father without being your real father. The 'real' part that counts has to do with love and care. If he loves you and cares for you, he is real. The love is real and the care is real, Tavis. You have a real daddy—that's the lesson. The blessing is that he never resented you or looked at you as anything other than his own. Your daddy is a blessing to you, and that's the truth, the biggest truth. And the truth is always a blessing."

As I cuddled next to Big Mama, she put her arm around me. And as she drifted off into a late-afternoon nap, so did I, my dreams a mixture of comfort and confusion.

I was disappointed that Mama didn't think I was mature enough to handle the truth. But I could feel the pain coursing through her. I could feel how hard it was for her to deal with her past life. It was a life she never discussed, a life she considered sinful. Her new life, the life into which she was born again, was the life she relished, the life that allowed her to live in the light.

A month or so after Mama's revelation, the family traveled in our rickety station wagon down to Gulfport to visit relatives and reconnect with our roots.

Elder Tate's Holiness church was rocking harder than ever. I loved being back in the world of Mississippi, where I could show my spirit in church without getting funny looks from the parishioners. We were back, said Mama, "in the bosom of the Lord."

Later that afternoon Mama and I walked down to the water's edge. We stopped to watch the sunset turn the sky copper gold.

"I wanted to spend some time alone with you today, Tavis, 'cause I wanted to ask you whether you want to meet T."

"When?"

"Right now. I called him and told him that you knew. He'd very much like to see you."

Half an hour later, Mom and I were walking up a path leading to the front door of a pretty, freshly painted house. A new Ford truck and a new Lincoln Town Car sat in the driveway. Mama rang the doorbell, and a tall thin man appeared. His voice was raspy, his manner cool.

"This is Tavis," Mama told the man. T offered his hand, and I shook it. His grip was strong.

"Tavis, this is T," Mama told me.

"Nice to meet you, sir," I said.

"Nice to meet you, Tavis. Come on in."

The living room was dark. In fact, the whole house was dark, giving it a sense of mystery. T turned on a lamp and invited me to sit on a leather couch. Mama sat next to me. T slid into an easy chair across from us.

My heart was beating loud enough that I was sure T could

hear it. I wanted to stare at T's face, to see if I recognized myself in him, but I knew that would be impolite. On the coffee table in front of me was a picture of a young girl. T noticed me looking at the photograph.

"That's your sister," he said.

His words hit me like a punch in the stomach. I had a sister I'd never met.

"No, I'm not her mother," Mama was quick to add to me. "T's had children with other women."

"Beautiful children," T confirmed. "You see, Tavis, you have a whole 'nother family here."

The idea excited me. The notion that I had sisters and brothers—an entire family I'd never met—blew my mind.

"Your mother tells me you're doing well at school up there in Indiana," said T.

"Tavis made the National Junior Honor Society," Mama announced.

"Is that so, son?" asked T.

I was struck by the sound of his voice when he said the word "son." It was no big deal; many older men call boys "son." It didn't have to mean anything. But it did: I *was* his son; *he* was my father. And yet we were strangers. Strangers or not, I was glad Mama mentioned the honor society. At that point, the society was the major accomplishment of my life. It was a *national* society, made up of kids from all over the country. I saw it as confirmation of Mrs. Graft's confidence in me. She had said I could compete with anyone anywhere, and I had proven her right.

"I like school," I said.

"He's a great reader and writer," Mom chimed in. "You should hear what his teachers say about him, T. You'd be proud."

"I am proud," T confirmed. "Real proud."

*Then why have I never heard from you?* I silently thought. *Or didn't you know about me? Why have I never seen you until now?*

"The teachers all talk about Tavis's verbal skills," Mom continued. "He also leads the young people's choir in church. Tavis has a beautiful voice. He's learning the Bible from Genesis to Revelation. We think he's going to be a sanctified preacher."

"Joyce," said T, "you've done a beautiful job with this boy. I feel a lot more peaceful now after meeting him."

My mind started racing: If T was proud of me, if T thought well of me, and if T had the money for a new truck, a new Lincoln, and a nice house, why didn't he ask me to live with him? I loved my dad Garnell, I loved Mama and Big Mama, and I loved my brothers and sisters. But in that moment I also loved the idea of not having to share a trailer with twelve other people, of having my own room and watching whatever I wanted to watch on TV—not to mention going to the movies, having my own backyard, not showing up at school with clothes too small and shoes with holes in the soles.

Was this why we'd come here? Did T want me to live with him? For several minutes I entertained the fantasy. But as I looked at Mama, I knew that was all it was—a fantasy. This man meant nothing to me. I would never give up Mama and my family for nicer clothes and my own bedroom.

Before long, our visit was over. When T got up to say goodbye, he didn't offer a "Come back and see me," or a "Please keep in touch," or an "I've got lots of room here and you're welcome to stay for as long as you like." He didn't even ask me to write him, or say, "I'll be keeping up with you through your mother." He just gave me a firm handshake. "Young man," said T, "I wish you the best."

"Thank you, T," Mama said to him. "This means a lot to me, and a lot to Tavis."

But as we left, I wondered, *What does it mean to me?*

I had met my father. But he wasn't my father. From that point forward, my biological father was out of my life forever.

Emory Garnell Smiley was waiting for us when we got back later that evening.

"Tavis," he said to me, "I know where your mother took you today, and I know it has to be a little confusing for you. All I can say is that I love you, and I always will. No one put a gun to my head to say that. No one put a gun to my head to care for you. I love you and care for you because, in my heart, you are my son."

My sense of family was reinforced when we went back home to Indiana by way of Georgia to visit Daddy's folks.

We called our grandma Mother Adel, and she was the sweetest woman in the world. She played church piano. We called our granddad Daddy Emory. Like our father, he was a tireless worker. He worked at the mill during the day. But at night and on weekends he ran the juke joint he'd built next to his house. Once again, the twin pillars of my family's African American culture—the spiritual and the secular—stood side by side in my grandparents' world of rural Georgia.

One Sunday, we all went to Mother Adel's church. The place rocked, and I was as happy as I could be. It was an all-day event where, as folks liked to say, *we had church*—a sermon that rolled like thunder, singers who soared, and Grandma Adel's rapid-fire piano that would have given Little Richard a run for his money.

After dinner, I heard music coming from the juke joint Daddy

Emory had built next door. Mama and Mother Adel were talking in the kitchen when I wandered out back. There was a window that looked into the juke joint, so I took a look. The women and men weren't just dancing, they were grinding to a song called "Who's Making Love to Your Old Lady While You Are Out Making Love?" Daddy Emory was selling moonshine out of a big jug. Everyone seemed to be smoking and drinking and laughing up a storm. Then Aretha came on the box, singing "Chain of Fools." The women formed a chain on one side, and the men made a chain on the other. The two chains started moving in on each other, the men and women pairing up in partners, switching off. Everyone was howling with delight. The smell of fried catfish and fried chicken made me hungry all over again.

"*Tavis!*" I heard Mama scream. "What are you doing out here, boy?"

"Nothing, ma'am."

"What you looking at?"

"Nothing."

"Looks like something to me," she said. "Like something you got no business seeing. Get back in the house."

And so I did.

Later in life, I've thought about the difference between my dad's life and his parents'. His father was not a churchgoer. His mother was. But her activities as a piano player were in the Baptist church. That was a lot different from the talking-in-tongues Pentecostal church of my mother. My mother wouldn't have tolerated a jukebox operation in a million years. Dancing was out. Drinking was out. Gutbucket blues was out.

Daddy went along with Mama. I think he realized that, given the strength of Mama's convictions, he had no choice. If the fam-

ily were to stay together—and above all, Dad was a family man—
he saw that it would have to do so within the confines of Mama's
believe-right church. Opposing her church would have provoked a
family crisis. And yet it was that very church that precipitated a
crisis greater than any of us could have imagined.

# In My Father's House

The church was packed for Sunday service, as it was every Sunday. My father and mother were now the leading lights of the New Bethel Tabernacle Church in Kokomo. They served on every possible committee. They were admired as model members. We, their children, were model church children.

This morning Elder Mills was talking about hellfire. He said that not enough preachers tell the truth about what happens when sinners don't repent and the devil prevails. "Hell is not a figment of our imagination. Hell is as real as rain. Except there is no rain in hell to extinguish the flames that burn forever. The agony goes on forever. The punishment is eternal. For all eternity, those who turn from our Lord, those who reject him, those who mock him, those who curse him or ignore him are doomed to live eternally without his comfort, love, and mercy. Hell is not a scene in a Hollywood movie. Hell is what awaits us when we turn from God's Word and God's grace. Brothers and sisters, hell is a four-letter word, a four-letter word that can haunt you and hurt you for the rest of your days and all the days to follow."

I appreciated Elder Mills's way with words. Words had become increasingly important to me. I saw how words were the measure of a man. Mom and Dad had great respect for Elder Mills's speeches, too. His cadences rose and fell like music. I didn't just follow those cadences, I felt them. At the same time, the thought of hell didn't frighten me, because if any family was going to avoid damnation, it was ours. We were the pride of the church.

I also wanted to be the pride of my school. But Mama and Daddy discouraged extracurricular activities like speech and drama. They wanted our extra time spent in church. As a result, I often felt cut off from the community around me. For all its piety, for all the saints who worshiped in its pews, for all its good intentions and devotion to the Word of God, our church isolated itself from the outside world. It shunned current dress. It shunned current culture—popular books, music, and movies. It even shunned athletics, because athletics were pursued in a secular environment. Our church wanted to protect us from the outside world. Mama and Dad agreed with this. Rather than live in the world, they felt it was better to live in church.

Thus, my great surprise on this particular Sunday when I heard a conversation between my dad and Douglas Hogan, our Sunday school supervisor, following the services.

"Brother Hogan," my dad said to him, "you have a minute?"

"Certainly do, Brother Smiley."

"Well, I was riding on Monroe Street last week when my station wagon hit a nasty pothole. Busted my tire and even busted the wheel."

Brother Hogan took out a pad and pen and got my father to give him the exact location of the pothole.

"You've got my word, Brother Smiley," he told my father, "that it'll be fixed by the end of the week. Those potholes are dangerous."

"Do you go out there and fix it yourself?" I asked him.

"Oh, no," he laughed. "We have a crew who does that."

"Brother Hogan is a councilman," my dad explained.

"What does a councilman do?" I asked.

"I tell you what, young man," Hogan responded, "why don't you come down to my office and I'll show you. Are you interested in local government?"

"Tavis is interested in everything," Dad explained.

"I like that," said Brother Hogan. "The more you want to learn, the more you do learn. I'll be waiting for your call, Tavis."


I called Brother Hogan the following week, and he invited me to his office.

I found Brother Hogan behind a desk with two phones that never seemed to stop ringing. A smaller desk stood on the other side of the room for his assistant, who had a phone of his own that rang just as constantly.

"Tavis," said Brother Hogan, "my assistant is out today. Would you mind answering his phone and seeing what they want?"

More excited than nervous, I picked up the receiver. "Councilman Hogan's office," I said.

"I need to speak to the councilman," a woman said.

"The councilman is on the other line. May I help you?"

"Yes, if you can figure out what happened to my Social Security check. It's two weeks overdue. I've called the Social Security office ten times, I've called my congressman another ten times, and

I'm tired of calling. If the check's lost, I need another one. My landlord is not a patient man. Can you do something for me?"

"One moment, ma'am."

I jotted down a note to Brother Hogan and handed it to him while he was on the phone with the mayor. He read the note, nodded, and scrawled the name and number of the head of the Social Security office in Indianapolis. "Call him, Tavis," he whispered out of the side of his mouth. "Take care of this."

Three phone calls later, I'd managed to locate the missing check and convince the Social Security office to special deliver it that afternoon. The woman was delighted. "You're a life saver," she said to me.

I was thrilled. I had no idea that someone high up in our church worked so intimately with city government. My gift of gab, even as a preteen, allowed me to talk confidently with people. Most of all, I was thrilled that I could actually help someone do what she couldn't do for herself. The notion of helping others came alive in me.

That afternoon I learned several things:

That I loved city government and its ability to come to people's aid.

That the idea of being an effective advocate was even more exciting than the prospect of becoming Tony Perez or Muhammad Ali or Michael Jackson.

That I needed to expand the concept of heroism beyond athletics or entertainment. A man like Brother Hogan was a real-life hero. Brother Hogan moved mountains for people who couldn't move them themselves. He changed the world where it really counted—in the lives of ordinary folks struggling to get by.

## "Shame on the Smileys!"

It started out like any other Sunday. Our trailer came to life at 7 A.M. Most of us boys had bathed the night before because there was never time for everyone to bathe on Sunday morning. We washed our faces, brushed our teeth, put on our Sunday best, and came to the breakfast table. Mama cooked up a full meal—grits, eggs, bacon, sausage, biscuits, the works. Mama was a great cook. She knew we needed fortification to get through an entire day of church.

I was in seventh grade. My linguistic skills were rapidly improving, and my confidence was building. I was doing well in my classes and eager to enter speech and debate competitions. Brother Hogan and our preacher, Elder Mills, encouraged me and acted as mentors, as did several teachers who engaged me in after-school discussions.

As we piled into the station wagon for the half-hour ride to church, I looked forward to Bible class. I'd been studying the book of John, our current focus for weeks, and was prepared to answer whatever questions popped up. The first student to give a correct answer got a piece of candy, and I liked winning candy. My only competition was my sister Phyllis. It became a question of who could raise his or her hand first.

For reasons I no longer remember, there was great excitement on this particular day. The kids in class were more energetic than usual, and our teacher, whom I'll call Sister W., seemed more frazzled. When she asked, "What is the new commandment described in John?," my hand went flying up. I answered, "That you love one another as I have loved you," adding, "John 13:34."

Several others knew the answer as well, including Phyllis, but my hand was up first, so I got the candy.

The more questions Sister W. asked, though, the more confused she appeared. If two or more of us raised our hands at the same time, she didn't know whom to call upon. In asking the questions, she often lost her place in the text. In responding to our answers, she seemed distracted. She was obviously having a bad day. Our class responded by giggling and acting a little unruly. Phyllis and I, however, always model students, remained quiet.

At a certain point, when Sister W. couldn't recall the last question she'd asked, she suddenly started crying and got up and left. We didn't understand why. It wasn't that she had lost control of the class; she had lost control of herself. We all watched as she dropped her notes and ran into Elder Mills's private office. We had no idea what was going on, but we were happy to have class dismissed early.

A half hour later I took my place on the second pew with my family. It was time for evening service. The Smileys were lined up like soldiers, dutiful servants of the Lord. We were all there except Mama, who was home resting. She had recently given birth to Scooter.

Soon we were all on our feet. We loved singing. With Dad and Big Mama shouting out the lyrics and us kids honing harmonies, our family practically had its own choir.

When Elder Mills began his sermon, I took out my Bible and turned to the passage he cited, 2 Timothy 1:7: "For God gave us not a spirit of fearfulness; but of power and love and discipline."

"Brothers and sisters," Elder Mills intoned, "I'm looking at this word 'discipline.' Without discipline there is no love because there is no order. Without discipline there is chaos, and within chaos is the character not of Christ but of the enemy. Only discipline will forestall the enemy. Only discipline will lead us to Christ. Only a few minutes ago I was told that during Children's Church today, discipline broke down. I was told that our own children were running wild, disobeying their teacher, disrespecting the sanctity of this building, and mocking the holy message being taught. I was further told, brothers and sisters, that the two culprits were Tavis and Phyllis. I have to say, shame on Tavis, shame on Phyllis, shame on the Smileys! When children disobey, it is usually not only their fault but also the fault of their parents. If parents can't keep their children from disrupting Children's Church, then something is very wrong. It is not our job here in church to teach discipline. Such discipline should—and must—be taught at home. I'm surprised and saddened that, in this regard, the Smiley family has not done its job. Brother Smiley, you're going to have to bring your children under control. I repeat, shame on the Smileys!"

I couldn't believe my ears. Phyllis and I looked at each other in shock. Elder couldn't be saying what he just said. I saw Dad's jaw tightening. The tension in our pew was unbearable. I could feel shame spread over us like a terrible rash. When the last hymn was sung and the closing prayer completed, we marched out of church, our heads hung low. We had been condemned, embarrassed, humiliated in front of the entire congregation.

In the car, Phyllis and I started to say that we hadn't done anything.

"Don't say another word!" Dad barked furiously. His tone was murderous. He refused to hear any words of explanation. Silence hung over us like a death sentence.

The trip home seemed to take forever. Both Phyllis and I knew what was ahead. We knew we were going to be whupped bad. The terrible thing was that we had done nothing wrong. Worse, we couldn't even argue our case.

Looking out the window at the cornfields, I considered jumping out of the car and hiding in those fields, running away, finding someplace in the vast landscape of Indiana where Dad could never find me.

When our station wagon pulled up to the trailer, both Phyllis and I got out and walked inside, awaiting our fate. Ten minutes passed; the waiting was unbearable.

Finally Daddy came in, looked at me and Phyllis, and said, "Go to the room." My heart sank.

I still wanted to tell my side of the story, but I knew I'd be slapped the minute I opened my mouth. I looked at Phyllis. Phyllis was braver than me. When it came to beatings, she always wanted to get it over with. "I'll go first," she said.

The entire family remained in the front of the trailer when Dad took Phyllis to the back bedroom. After a few seconds, the screams began. We'd all heard crying before—we were used to it—but nothing like this. Phyllis's screams were horrendous, and they went on and on. Before long, the screams became bloodcurdling. My siblings looked at me with shocked expressions in their eyes, as if to ask, *What is he doing to her? Is he killing her?*

Finally, the screams subsided. All we could hear was Phyllis whimpering.

"Tavis!" Daddy's voice boomed from the far end of the trailer. "Get in here!"

His murderous rage had not subsided. I walked slowly to the back bedroom, scared to death. When I opened the door, Dad was standing there with an extension cord in his right hand. In the past, when we were whipped, it was usually with a switch. I'd never been whipped with an extension cord before. Now I understood why Phyllis's screams had sounded so tortured.

"Turn around, Tavis," he said.

For the next several minutes, my father brutally beat me, his red rage overtaking his common sense. The extension cord tore into my flesh. My backside was ripped into open, stripped ribbons of blood. The blinding pain was like nothing I had ever experienced. I cried in agony, anger, fear. I couldn't stop crying, even when he, breathing heavily, was finally through. I couldn't stop even as I stumbled out of the bedroom and saw the panicked eyes of my younger brothers, traumatized by what Daddy had done.

When I got to the bedroom I shared with Garnie, I couldn't manage to climb to the upper bunk, where I usually slept. My limbs didn't have the strength. When I tried to remove my blood-stained shirt, the blood and torn skin from the open wounds stuck to the fabric. Shedding my shirt was an excruciating ordeal. When I looked at my back and legs in the mirror, all I saw was blood and pieces of skin. I couldn't touch it with hot water or towels; the pain was too intense. Nor could I get in bed. In the end, I couldn't do anything but stand there.

Mama came in a little while later. When she looked at me, she started crying, praying, "Oh, Jesus, dear Jesus, help us, Jesus." Normally I loved hearing Mama pray. But this time her prayers held no power over me, offered no salve or comfort. When she touched my hand, when she touched my face, I turned away. Silently, I accused her, *You knew he was out of control. Why didn't you stop him? Why did you let him do this?*

Hours later, the pain was still so excruciating that I was unable to lie in bed. Half-awake, half-asleep, I spent the night on my feet. When morning came, it stung like a swarm of hornets to even touch my back with a wet towel. On the bus to school neither Phyllis nor I leaned back in our seats. Phyllis was worse off than me. Forbidden to wear pants, her legs were exposed, and her cuts were visible. Mine were hidden beneath my shirt and pants. I wanted to say something to her, commiserate with her in some way, but I didn't know what to say. My heart was filled with sadness, anger, pain. I wanted to run away. I never wanted to see my mother and father again.

Gym class that morning was an ordeal. We were usually required to change into shorts and a T-shirt, but I refused to take off my clothes. I didn't want to expose myself. So I just sat on the bench in the locker room. When our gym teacher noticed me, he said, "Get dressed, Tavis." By now all my classmates were dressed and staring at me.

"I can't, sir," I said.

"Why not?"

"I'm not feeling well."

"What do you mean?"

"I'm just not feeling good."

"Do you have a note from your parents excusing you from gym?"

"No, sir."

"Then get dressed. Now."

"No, sir. I can't."

"You have no choice, Tavis. Come on, you'll be all right." Before I could move away, he patted me on the back. The second he touched me, I screamed in agony and jumped away.

"My God, son," he said, "what's wrong?"

"Nothing," I said, grimacing.

"Did someone hurt you?"

"No, sir," I lied. But something within me broke wide open, and I started crying.

"I'm taking you to the nurse's office, Tavis," the teacher said. "Something's very wrong here."

In the nurse's office, with the coach and assistant principal looking on, I was forced to peel off my shirt.

The school officials gasped.

"Who did this?" the assistant principal asked me.

When I told them my daddy had punished me, he asked, "Did he beat anyone else?"

"My sister Phyllis," I told him. The next thing I heard, Phyllis was being called out of class.

With Phyllis sitting by my side in the nurse's office, I heard the nurse calling the medical emergency people. Next, I heard the assistant principal calling Children's Protective Service. I was in a daze.

A short time later, the county sheriff arrived. And not long after that, Phyllis and I were being taken to the hospital, where we remained for the next several days.

Our lives would never be the same again.

# The Boxcar Children

The scars of that beating were worse for Phyllis than for me. She was hit so hard on her calves and thighs that she carries those marks to this day. My skin was tougher, or perhaps Daddy had vented the worst of his rage on my sister; in any event, eventually my wounds healed. Emotionally, in the wake of our beatings, Phyllis became angry and rebellious at my parents. I rebelled too, but in less obvious ways.

My last day in the hospital, the little black-and-white TV across from my bed was on the blink. Most of the news in the preceding week concerned the upcoming election—the sitting president Ford, trying to rally the Republican faithful in the aftermath of Watergate and Nixon's resignation, versus Democratic challenger Jimmy Carter. But my mind was a million miles away from politics and world events.

My parents visited me every day. They apologized profusely, ashamed at what their actions had brought about. But I wasn't interested in anything they had to say. I remained as silent as a stone statue. When they tried to look me in the eye or touch my arm or shoulder to try to bridge the emotional chasm between us, I turned away.

I was still in a state of shock and still in great pain. I was in no position to deal with them on any terms. I was angry at my father for doing what he did and disappointed with my mother for not stopping him. I instinctively knew what all youngsters know: that regardless of the circumstances, children are entitled to justice. Children are entitled to a fair hearing. Children are supposed to be kept safe. I realize now that that was one of the great lessons of that horrific incident—regardless of anyone's age, false accusations leave deep psychological wounds that take years to heal, if indeed they ever do heal. Now I see that clearly; back then I could only respond to my parents' attempt to apologize by acting as though they didn't exist. My rage took the form of a terrible silence. And because I was an incessant talker, my silence was the loudest and most effective message I could send.

My brother Garnie came to visit me, bringing my favorite book, *The Boxcar Children*. It was a book I'd been reading and rereading since I was nine years old. Now more than ever the book spoke to me about my own experiences, my own loneliness.

In the book, four young children—Henry, Jessie, Violet, and Benny—are orphaned, lost in the world. Henry, the oldest, becomes the head of their makeshift household. I related to Henry. I fantasized about a parentless life. I loved how the four kids discover an abandoned railroad boxcar, which they turn into their home. I saw how the boxcar was similar to our own home in the trailer. I admired Henry's independence and resourcefulness; he and his siblings build a dam across a brook and create a pool deep enough for swimming. I was moved by this adventure story of kids surviving without a mother or a father, kids caring for themselves in an alien world. In the end, a good-hearted doctor finds the children and unites them with their wealthy and kindly grandfather. They live happily ever after—without the benefit, or complication, of parents.

A man from the Children's Protective Service came to my hospital bed that day, asking, "Do you want to return to your parents?" He explained that legal proceedings were under way involving my parents. I could go home if I wanted, or I could be placed with foster parents.

"I don't want to go home," I said. "I don't want to see my parents."

I was still scared that my parents would beat me. Having embarrassed them by being sent to the hospital, I was frightened that they would take that embarrassment out on me. I had tried to keep the beating under wraps; I had tried to avoid undressing during gym class so the teachers wouldn't know; I had done all I could to ensure that our family's privacy was not invaded. But I had failed and was scared that Mama and Dad would punish me even further. After all, I humiliated them in public. I got them into even more trouble. Who knew the extent of their wrath? If my father's rage was great before, it might be even greater now. I couldn't take a chance. I couldn't go home.

Thinking about my father, I was deeply confused by what had happened. Daddy wasn't the one who flew into rages in our family; Mama was. Daddy was the one who never flared up or lost his cool. Daddy was the one who, with open arms, had taken in four extra kids. Daddy had taken in his mother-in-law. Daddy had taken in *me*, a child Mama had had with another man. Yet this man who showed so much character was the same man who had put me in the hospital. How was I to make sense of it all?

The local newspaper carried the news of our beating and the pending legal proceeding against my father. Everyone in our church knew. Everyone in school knew. Everyone at the Grissom Air Force Base knew. The scandal had turned a spotlight on our entire family. I couldn't escape the scandal. None of us could. And I didn't know how to deal with it. My embarrassment was the deepest I had ever felt.

Much later, as an adult tempered by many seasons of rejection, I can see there are three things that everyone wants in life: love, respect, and attention. In the aftermath of the beatings, I felt the absence of my parents' love, I felt the absence of their respect (they still hadn't asked me to address or answer the minister's accusation), and I felt the absence of the right kind of attention. I was emotionally devastated.

In the end, Phyllis was sent away to live in a white foster home in Peru, Indiana, a few miles away. She was so scarred by what had happened that she never went back to the trailer.

Ironically, I was assigned to a foster home of an elderly black preacher and his wife who lived in a trailer on the opposite end of our trailer park.

I was desperate for my family not to know my whereabouts, for fear they'd persuade me to come back. When I was driven to my foster family's trailer, I put my head down on the backseat so I wouldn't be seen by my siblings or parents.

My world had been turned upside down. A week before, I had been part of a family of ten children. Now, I had become an only child. A week before, I had shared a bedroom with three other brothers. Now, I suddenly had a bedroom of my own. A week before, I could seldom watch television. Now, I could watch whatever I wanted. A week before, I was a standout student and choir member of my church; now, I knew other kids would whisper about me at school, and I would worship with strangers in a strange church.

Less than a mile separated the trailer of my family and the trailer of my foster family. But that distance represented the difference between my old life and my new one.

The emotional turmoil inside me—the outrage and humiliation, the confusion and pain, the determination to get even with my parents, and the yearning for their love—overwhelmed me. It was a part of me every minute of every day.

How would I keep from falling apart?

# A Rage That Reaches to Heaven

Preparing for my first day at my foster father's church, I came upon this phrase in 2 Chronicles: "a rage that reaches to heaven." The phrase seemed to describe my own anger at my family and the world. Rage at Sister W. for having a nervous breakdown at Phyllis's and my expense. Rage at Elder Mills for not looking at our side of the story despite our record of involvement and good works in church. Rage at Daddy for beating us so brutally without even listening to what we had to say. Rage at Mama for letting him hurt us. Even rage at God.

Everyone seemed to have snapped that Sunday: our teacher, our preacher, our parents. They were all God-fearing adults. Shouldn't the Spirit of God have intervened? Shouldn't the wisdom and teachings of the Bible have interceded on our behalf? Shouldn't God have protected us against such injustice?

The thing I loved most—my family—had been torn apart. The two people I loved and respected the most—Mama and Daddy—had shattered my trust and respect for them. My whole framework of thinking, my view of the world—that teachers and preachers and parents know best—had been overturned.

In my moral universe, God himself had come under challenge.

But no matter how strong my rage, I was incapable of not attending Sunday school at my foster father's Baptist church in Peru.

My new routine felt strange and unsettling. Getting up Sunday morning, I was grateful that none of my brothers had peed on me during the night. It dawned on me that I could take as much time in the bathroom as I wanted. The trailer, which was as big as the Smiley trailer, housed only three people, not thirteen. My foster father and mother were quiet people. There was little noise, no kids yelling, no parents shouting and chastising, no desperate rushing to get ready.

My new foster parents told me they were glad to share their home with a well-spoken boy who knew the Bible. On the drive to Peru, they assured me that I'd like their parishioners and that the parishioners would like me.

When we entered church, I felt every eye focused on me. My foster dad introduced me to his deacons. He couldn't have been more gracious. I took my seat in the first pew. I knew that everyone knew my story and that I was likely viewed with a degree of pity. And I knew that, despite everyone's friendliness, being a stranger in a strange church did not mitigate the shame.

My foster father preached that morning as if he'd read my mind.

"When the old song says, 'Jesus is a friend of mine,' I take it personally because Jesus is a personal messiah. He brings God to us. He *is* God, but God in the body of a man who can feel what we feel. You talk to Jesus like you talk to a sure-enough pal. Tell him you're happy or sad, afraid or confused. Speak your heart and he hears you not only with a beautiful understanding but with ears—God's divine ears—that have healing power. When you talk to Jesus and Jesus listens, you're changed. We praise him, yes, and praising feels good, but there's nothing wrong with telling him that you're angry, that life isn't treating you the way you wanna be treated. Don't hold back when you speak to the Lord. He is God Almighty, but he is also down-home. He'll come to your home, he'll come to your heart, he'll be there when you call his name. My point is simple: You don't have to pretend with Jesus. You don't have to put on airs. You don't have to act like everything is rosy. Jesus' divine humanness connects to our humanness. He can deal with your anger. He can deal with anything you got. So don't hold back. Give it to him. Let our precious Lord know exactly what you're going through. Remember, friends, he was ambushed; he was betrayed; he was falsely accused; he was tortured; he was mur- dered—and all for your sake. All to reconcile you to the Father. All to represent you and love you and give you life eternal. He can take away your burdens—your shame, your restless mind, your heartache, and your pain. He is the Good Doctor, whose bedside manner is nothing short of miraculous. So like the song says, 'Pre- cious Lord, take my hand.' Let him lead you. Let him calm you. Let him give you the love and peace that you can only find in the sanctity of the Trinity, where Father, Son, and Spirit all come to- gether as one. In the precious name of Jesus, amen."

The words hit home with me. Just because I was angry with God didn't mean I didn't love God. If I felt God had let me down, that didn't mean God didn't love me. For God is constant, steady, I realized. He takes me the way I am. He forgives me, changes me. I couldn't live my life without God. I knew the world could be cruel—I had experienced it firsthand. The world throws us curve- balls, trips us up, persecutes us, confounds and confuses us. That's just the world. But God is above the world, as well as in the world.

He is everything we can and cannot see. God is love. When Sister W. flipped out, or when Elder Mills unjustly accused us, or when my dad went berserk, they weren't God. Sitting there in my foster father's church, I realized that Sister W. and Mills and Dad were just people who had gone a little crazy.

Nonetheless, the anger at those who had wronged me remained. It would not go away for a long, long time. Faith was one thing—I discovered I'd never really lost it. But forgiveness was another—and at this point, I just didn't have it in me.

"Did you like the sermon?" my foster mom asked on the ride back from Peru to Bunker Hill.

"Yes, ma'am," I answered.

"I knew you'd enjoy church," she said. "We're proud to have you with us, son."

Just as her comforting words washed over me, I saw that we were about to enter the trailer park. In the distance I saw my brothers out in the field playing baseball. My heart started beating like crazy. Man, how I yearned to join them! But I ducked down instead, afraid they'd spot me, afraid I'd be drawn back to a household I could no longer abide.

Over time, my anger became tinged with a new emotion—loneliness. Being one of ten children, I had never known what loneliness was before. I never imagined I'd ever be lonely. Fact is, if I fantasized at all, it was about being an only child. And now I was.

# Despising the Shame

According to Hebrews, Jesus endured the cross, "despising the shame," and thus was set down at the right hand of God.

"Despising the shame." It was a phrase that resonated deep within me. For shame haunted my days, my nights, my dreams.

When I returned to school after over two weeks' absence, I saw my classmates looking at me with unease and pity, knowing what had happened. But rather than despising or throwing off the shame, I felt it running through me. I was ashamed when articles appeared in the paper about my dad. I was ashamed when my classmates ridiculed me for wearing last year's clothes. I was ashamed when I overheard someone say something about my "crazy parents."

For all my desire to punish Mama and Daddy, I missed my family. I missed my sisters and brothers, missed the fun we had and the family fellowship that could never be replaced. For the first time in my life, I was without the people I loved and who loved me. And though I was only a mile away, it felt like I was living on another continent.

To be sure, my foster parents doted on me, and I deeply appreciated their care and concern. But at dinnertime, I couldn't help thinking of what Mama might be making. I would think of her meat loaf or her delicious smothered chicken. Mom's cooking was one of the highlights of my day—or at least used to be. My foster mom made nutritious meals, but, God bless her, her cooking just couldn't hold a candle to Mama's.

From the outside, you'd think my life as an only child was perfect. I'd never had it so good. My new home was a vast improvement over my life in the Smiley trailer, where every day was an ongoing accommodation of the needs and feelings of others.

Yet I was now seeing that an only child's life was lonely, particularly when you're used to a family that spills over into every part of your existence. I was used to endless noise, jostling for position, competing for attention, the companionship of a gaggle of siblings every moment of every day. I found myself missing Garnie and Scooter, Maury and Dubby, Dion and Patrick and Paul as if part of me had been cut out and removed. I wondered about Phyllis. How was she doing? I missed my sister Pam.

I lived away from the Smiley trailer for four or five months, growing lonelier by the day. Because I was in junior high and my brothers were in elementary, I didn't encounter them at school. My sister Pam was in high school and Phyllis was attending an entirely different school. So I had no contact with anyone. When I was with my foster family in the trailer park, I stayed to myself. But it couldn't last forever.

One Saturday afternoon, after finally finishing my homework for the weekend and completing my Sunday school lesson, I was feeling restless. The air outside was a little chilly, but not chilly enough to prevent some of the boys from playing baseball. It had been so long since I'd played. Why not wander outside and watch?

As I walked toward the field, I saw my brothers in the distance. Suddenly my heart was ready to burst. They were in the middle of a game. When they saw me coming toward them, they started waving like crazy.

"Tavis!" they yelled.

"It's Tavis!"

"Where you been hiding, Tavis?"

"When you coming home, Tavis?"

I tried to answer their questions, but then I stopped. Instead I asked a question of my own. "Anyone playing first base?"

"You," said Garnie. "You're our first baseman."

And just like that I trotted out on the field and took my position. It felt so good to be back, playing the game I loved with the brothers I loved.

We played a great game. We pounded the ball and beat the daylights out of the other team, making impossible circus catches, laying down perfect bunts, striking out batters. In miraculous fashion, we found our form. The Smiley boys were back.

When the game was over, daylight began to fade. There was an awkward pause between us. *What happens now?*

As my brothers gathered up the bats, balls, and gloves, they looked over to me.

Finally Garnie asked, "Coming home, Tavis?"

A simple question.

*Coming home, Tavis?*

If I go home, I wondered, does it mean I've capitulated? Does it let Dad and Mom off the hook? Does it mean that what they did to me was okay? Where do I put my anger?

While I couldn't put my anger aside, neither could I watch my brothers walk away from me. So I walked with them.

When we arrived at our trailer, I let my brothers go in first. Then I walked up the steps, opened the door and walked inside. Mama and Daddy were in the kitchen. Mama was peeling potatoes. Dad was fixing a clogged sink. When they saw me come in, they stopped what they were doing.

They looked at me wordlessly with love, with shame, with a question in their eyes. I looked at them quickly and averted my eyes. What was I doing here? I wondered. What did all this mean? But I didn't leave. In fact, I stayed the night, sandwiched between my brothers, competing for bed space.

The next day, after services at my foster father's church, I moved back home.

My siblings acted as though I'd never left, but my parents said very little to me when I walked into the trailer with my bags. It was as though they assumed I'd be back eventually. They knew what I knew—what, in fact, my siblings and grandmother knew—that I loved my family, heart and soul.

When I told my foster parents of my decision, they were understanding. They saw I'd been lonely for my real family. And as for Mama and Daddy, I could feel their relief to have me back. I don't say this to brag, but I have a big personality, and I could sense that the absence of my personality left a hole in the family. Moreover, the longer I was gone, the guiltier my father felt. He didn't say that in so many words, but I could read between the lines. After all, it was his actions that had resulted in two of his kids leaving.

———

Although I'd returned home, I hadn't returned the same as I was before I left. My rage lived on, as did my humiliation.

I knew that for better or worse, my family was where I had to be. But the months of living with my foster family had only reinforced the pain I felt. Mama and Dad had both apologized, but didn't do anything special to make it up to me. I understood that. With nine other kids in the house, they had to keep things balanced. They couldn't make one child feel more or less important than another.

So I returned to my parents' house, ate their food, obeyed their rules, but did not reengage with them emotionally. I refused to ask for their advice or help. I found myself speaking to them only when I was spoken to. I gave them as little of myself as I could, locking them out of my heart.

In the end, my father had been neither punished nor jailed for the beatings. I wasn't in the courtroom the day of his trial. I later learned, however, that the judge had already listened to a dozen cases where the parents were accused of being negligent of their children.

"When the judge came to our case," Dad told us all that night, "he saw that I had overreacted, but he also saw that your mother and I were concerned parents who were completely involved in our children's lives and well-being. Compared to the other cases he had heard, where the parents didn't know or care what was happening with their kids, we were seen in a good light. The judge warned us that parents shouldn't punish when they're enraged. I agreed; I'd learned my lesson. But he also complimented us for keeping our kids at home, in school, and in church and out of the criminal justice system."

I betrayed little reaction to my father's report. On the one hand, I didn't want him incarcerated—I loved him, and a harsher punishment would only add to the notoriety and shame. But I also couldn't forgive him for what had happened. I just couldn't dismiss the beating I had received as a minor misdemeanor or mistake. It hadn't happened in a moment of blind rage, but rather a rage that had been formed and fueled over an hour or two. Worst of all was the sense of betrayal I felt at the hands of my parents. I had respected them, and they had betrayed my trust. The humiliation I felt redefined my attitude toward the outside world; it would fundamentally reshape my character. I know in my heart even today that had my sister Phyllis and I not been beaten that night, we would have grown up differently, into different people.

My inner world shifted in the wake of the beatings. From that day forward, I learned to trust my own truth, rather than Mom's or Dad's. My parents were my parents, but God would be the only one I would trust to carry me through. I was determined to spend as much time as necessary putting distance between me and this humiliation, me and this memory, me and this poverty we lived in. I was determined to do that by making a good name for myself, by making an impression on the world. I was determined to live down the shame I felt by rising above it.

I now know—thirty years after the fact—that processing anger takes as long as it takes. You can't rush it. You can't wash or wish it away. You have to live with it and live through it. Out of that anger, though, another bit of wisdom emerged: no ties are stronger than family. Nothing, not even the bite of a brutal and unfair beating, could break that tie. I needed my family. And in the end, despite everything, I simply didn't want to live without them.

# Turn the Fear to Energy

It wasn't until college that I began appreciating the greatness of artists like Curtis Mayfield and Marvin Gaye. My middle school and high school years—with one life-altering exception—were defined for the most part by white culture. I knew of Martin Luther King Jr., but knew relatively little about black culture and civil rights and the outside world. Hank Aaron was my hero among baseball players, Ali in the world of boxing. I knew nothing of Malcolm X. There was no way I could have been schooled in African American culture in the middle of white Indiana.

Later I would learn that Marvin Gaye had written a song called "Ego Tripping Out" that contains the words "Turn the fear to energy."

I'm not sure I would have understood that concept as a teenager. But that's exactly the approach I took to life. Fear drove me to excel. As a young boy from a black family, living hand to mouth in a cramped trailer home, I constantly found myself asking, Was I good enough? Was I smart enough?

My lack of self-esteem was palpable. I suffered from the insecurity of being black in an overwhelmingly white community, from being poor, from being from a large family where competition for attention and affection was fierce. Unconsciously, I began to turn that fear of being poor, of being "less than," into outsized motivation. I became tenacious in my studies. I became ambitious in setting goals. I turned my fear into an excessive striving for excellence. Truth be told, the energy unleashed by my humiliation is still one of the dominant underlying forces driving me. I learned to use fear to forge ahead rather than hide, to use uncertainty to plunge into rather than avoid life, to move forward no matter what.

When I returned to school after the scandal, I was driven to show everyone around me that I was as good as, if not better than, they were. I was determined to show them that I could win at whatever contest I entered. I'd redeem myself, and my family, by blasting my way into a heroic future. I was determined to shine.

Phyllis reacted very differently, perhaps because she was older or because she was a girl. Whatever the reason, her path was not easy; she rebelled with a vengeance and fell into a lifestyle of drugs and addiction that nearly did her in. She had children out of wedlock and got hooked on crack. Thankfully, she survived, recovered, and is doing well today. But the scars that she carried on her body broke her spirit for decades to follow.

My own spirit was surely bruised, but it wasn't crushed. Why was I able to take this low point in my life and transform it into the start of something new? How was I able to turn the fear into energy?

I'd like to say it was faith in God, and surely God was, is, and will always be the center of my spiritual life. But the truth is that, even though I went back to Elder Mills's church and sat with my family on the second pew, it wasn't divine revelation that kept me on the straight and narrow. It was the burning desire to show my peers, my teachers, Elder Mills, and my parents that I could be successful, that I could overcome the pain and injustice that weighed so heavily on my heart.

My transformation didn't happen overnight. Eighth grade was rough. I hadn't found my footing; I was still living in a haze. My forward momentum hadn't kicked in yet. I was back in the trailer, back with the Smiley & Sons cleaning crew, back into an every-evening-in-church routine.

I was looking for the arena in which I could excel. I was a good athlete, but not a great one. I was a good singer, but not the best around. I was a good writer, but others wrote better. So what was my strongest point? Where was I most confident, able to compete with anyone? What was my strength and natural talent?

Talking.

I discovered I had a way with words. They came easily to me. I felt comfortable talking, confident, even powerful. The sound of sentences rolling out in conversation gave me a feeling like nothing else. Some guys could throw a football the length of a field; some could sit at the piano and riff like Ray Charles; others could solve mathematical mysteries in the blink of an eye. I could talk.

Mrs. Graft was the first to see my ability. "You have a good mind, Tavis," she had told me in grade school, "and you express yourself beautifully. You're highly verbal; you don't have to feel inferior to anyone."

Years later in our church I had met Brother Hogan, a black man who saw my innate ability and encouraged me, hiring me to work in his office. As a city councilman, he understood the extraordinary power of communication.

"The best representation of yourself," he said, "are the words you speak. If you can communicate with people, people immediately respect you. There's no telling how far you can go with good communication."

Nonetheless, communication at home with my parents practically ceased. I suppose it was my way of letting them know that the hurt they had caused me hadn't gone away. It was my way of continuing to punish them.

"How was school today?" Mama would ask.

"Fine," I'd answer flatly.

"Anything interesting happen?"

"No."

"You have homework?"

"Yes."

"Well, get it done."

And with that, I was on my own. Dinnertime, as far as I was concerned, was a stone-silent affair. I said not a word to either Mama or Daddy. I would answer their occasional questions by nodding my head yes or shaking my head no.

I realized that it frustrated and angered my parents, and in my heart I was secretly glad.

In church, I gave Elder Mills the same treatment. If he asked me a question, I'd answer him with ice-cold brevity that conveyed how little use I had for him.

In short, I was like two different people—extremely outgoing and talkative in school, and silent at home and in church. In school, I used my verbal ability to engage others; at home and in church, my silence made it clear that I was still seething inside.

Growing up, I lived in provinces within provinces. Kokomo, Peru, and Bunker Hill were all small, provincial towns in a rela-

tively provincial state. Our middle and senior high school, Maconaquah, was across the street from a huge cornfield. And within
the tiny African American community in our part of the state, our
church was even more provincial. Like Hasidic synagogues where
ultraorthodox Jews cut themselves off from the modern world surrounding them, the New Bethel Tabernacle Church was a self-
contained province.

Yet I had links to the wider world. They might have been few
in number, but they would prove to be the keys to my future, my
way of tackling the challenges and complexities of the larger
world. Councilman Hogan was such a link, a black man and member of our Holiness church who nonetheless operated in the realm
of everyday politics. Another link to the outside world in our
church was Deacon James Gossett.

"Here, Tavis," Deacon Gossett said to me one Sunday, out of
the blue. "I'd like you to have these."

He handed me a collection of long-playing albums on the Mo-
town label. But what he handed me wasn't music by the Supremes
or the Temptations; it wasn't the Four Tops or Little Stevie Wonder. It was a series of speeches by Martin Luther King Jr. I don't
know why Deacon Gossett gave me those records. Perhaps he
knew I was taking speech classes in school. Or perhaps he felt that
I would relate to the substance and style of Dr. King and his
speeches.

Those speeches rocked my world.

The provincial walls I lived within had already begun to
crumble.

The lesson I learned, one of the most valuable of my life, was
an obvious one: Find your talent and go with it. Figure out what
you're good at and develop it. The more you honor and hone that

talent, the further you'll go. The more you neglect it, the less it will serve you. Talent is a precious commodity. Once you identify yours, cherish it, cultivate it, practice it.

If my talent was talking, then, believe me, no one was going to shut me up.

# America Has Defaulted

Over the next few years, I would often sit on the floor in the living room of our trailer, my father's headphones pressed to my ears. Dad had given me permission to use the phonograph, a rare privilege in our family. Dad's precious phonograph was normally off limits. He made an exception only because he respected Deacon Gossett and saw no harm in the sermons of Dr. King.

I checked out a book of Dr. King's speeches from our school library, one of the few books I could find concerning African Americans. Now in ninth grade, I was enrolled in speech class, preparing for a series of speech contests. They triggered my intensely competitive spirit. I was searching for just the right material, and after listening to Dr. King for only a minute or two, I knew I had found a kindred spirit.

It was a stormy afternoon when I made my discovery, simultaneously reading the text of King's speeches while listening to his mellifluous voice on my father's phonograph. Mama was baking cakes in the kitchen at the time, and the aroma was sweet. The crackle of distant thunder and the radio report of possible torna-does had me on edge. I looked out the window and saw that the sky—half dark, half light—had the right disposition for twisters. A sense of danger hung in the air. That same ominous threat of sud-den change thundered in the sound of Dr. King's voice. I felt the ge-nius of King's soul. His radical politics would take time for me to grasp, but the musicality of his phrases seduced me from the first sentence.

I remember my siblings were running around the trailer. Big Mama was helping my mom in the kitchen, while Dad was tinker-ing with his car outside. With the headphones clamped against my ears, though, I was oblivious to it all. I was lost in the magic of King's language, five-hundred miles away in the National Mall in Washington, D.C., amid a teeming crowd of supporters. I imag-ined looking up at the podium placed before the Lincoln Memor-ial where Dr. King was speaking. The date was August 28, 1963, the year before my birth. In some ways, listening to Dr. King's speech and imagining myself at the great March on Washington *was* my birth, at least my rebirth, my christening into a larger world where words and ideas fired my imagination and excited my ambitions.

"I have a dream," Dr. King intoned. In English class, we were just starting to learn about similes, metaphors, and figures of speech. Those concepts weren't immediately clear to me as Dr. King talked about "symbolic shadow," but when he spoke of com-ing to Washington to "cash a check," when he said the founding fathers had signed a "promissory note to which every American was to fall heir" and that "America has defaulted," I understood the power of symbolic language. When he claimed that America "has given the Negro people a bad check, a check which has come back marked 'insufficient funds,' " I saw how metaphors could stir the heart and persuade the mind. Dr. King spoke in the cadences of the black church in which I'd been raised. I loved those cadences. His was a familiar voice, a preacher's voice, an evangelist's voice, though grander and more eloquent than any I'd ever heard.

Over the next several weeks, I spent hours studying that one speech. I would recite it in unison with Dr. King, memorizing every nuance, noting how he emphasized a certain vowel or consonant. I'd stand before the mirror and elongate words and modulate my inflections as he did.

But such practice also contained a metaphysical component. King's speeches touched me so deeply and profoundly that, for reasons I couldn't explain, I found myself crying. I wasn't sure what those tears represented. Maybe his words touched the pain and hurt and humiliation I was still feeling. Maybe my tears stemmed from the new confidence and purpose his words gave me. Maybe I felt an empathy with my people, whose history of suffering and survival was coming alive to me for the first time. In part, they reflected my pride in the courageous brilliance of a leader outspoken in conveying our purpose and passion.

I see now that King influenced me on several levels. First, he showed me that words have meaning—they aren't arbitrary—and words are powerful. He showed me that words can carry the force of love. He also showed me that one man can make a difference. He himself had made that difference. Plus he demonstrated great love for his people. I myself felt that love; expressed in his words and the testimony of his life, that love was powerfully validated. King also personified self-determination. I hooked onto that concept. I hooked onto the notion that we were to be positive, forward looking, and progressive. Hope was his mantra; hope was his conviction. Despite evidence to the contrary, King believed that things would get better. Every day that I read his words, they moved me like a powerful sermon. They changed my life and emboldened my ambition.

Though Dr. King had passed on long before I encountered his remarkable spirit, I got to know the man better than I knew most of my teachers. I knew him through his words. He spoke to me, and I spoke to him. In a mystical but decidedly practical sense, he became my mentor.

The lesson to me is clear. There is a world of righteous mentors available to each of us. We can adopt them. We can live with them through their words. We can communicate with them as surely as we communicate with our parents and friends. We can keep them close to us as long as we live. Even as I write this, I feel Dr. King by my side.

Maconaquah, our town high school, went from grades nine through twelve. The student body was 98 percent white, kids of white farmers and military personnel. There was a sprinkling of sons and daughters of migrant Mexicans who worked the tomato and cornfields. Like the air-force people, they kept transferring and moving on to new lands and new schools. They'd come and go with the seasons. I related to the Mexicans, who usually had little skill in English, and went out of my way to befriend them. As one of the few black students at Maconaquah, I understood the challenges of being part of a distinct minority.

The paradox, though, was that in the ultrawhite culture of Bunker Hill's school system, I became an academic star. These four years were the happiest of my life. Some people, being from a different race and culture, might experience these years as a constant cultural clash and see themselves as outsiders. I was able to embrace it as cultural confluence. As one of the lone black people, I stood out. It was easier for me to gain recognition. And in the competitive arena of speech contests, I was able to take the words of Dr. King and use them to overwhelm my competition.

So dramatic was the growth in my confidence in high school that I ran for ninth-grade student council. It was my first foray into elected politics. I liked putting myself on the line. I busily gathered groups of supporters and devoted several days to preparing posters that I plastered all over school. There were no issues to be debated. It was a pure popularity contest, and I was determined to charm the electorate. The fact that my parents would not be pleased if I won motivated me even more. They were skeptical of all non-church extracurricular activities. My growing oratorical skills helped others to see me as an articulate student who would represent our class with dignity and intelligence.

When I won, I was jubilant. I took my place as a leader among my peers. And somehow, it felt natural and right. I was on my way. I didn't know where I was going, but any movement forward was better than no movement at all.

# High School Hierarchy

Most high schools are filled with social cliques. They are stratified on practically every level. Mine was no different. High school is a time when we are at our most vulnerable, most needy. We are subject to powerful positive and negative influences. It is a time when hormones kick in with a vengeance, when we're overwhelmed with sexual energy, when we're poised to go in one direction or another.

Our high school in Bunker Hill consisted of poor farm boys in denim overalls; sons and daughters of air-force colonels and captains wearing crisp, clean Izod shirts; wholesome all-American cheerleaders; rednecks driving pickups with gun racks in the back; jocks, geeks, and nerds.

Where was my place in all this? Where did I belong?

All my friends were white. But oddly enough, I couldn't hang out with them. That's because Mama's church prohibited my going to parties and even sporting events. Occasionally, my parents would let me visit Doug McCoy, a white friend of mine. Doug had a great relationship with his family. Seeing how peaceful and calm things were at Doug's house showed me how different home life could be.

But while I couldn't see my friends outside of school, at school I became the man. I was respected and liked. Reading Dr. King's speeches about how we could get along, I *was* getting along. I *was* being judged not by the color of my skin but by the content of my character. I *was* living out part of the dream that King had so vividly described.

I was determined to be viewed as a winner, but I had to win without a car, without cool clothes, without a house where I could invite friends, without the ability to date girls—and without achieving notoriety as the lead singer for a rock-'n'-roll band or the star quarterback.

"We're going for the win," I remember our speech coach telling us. "We're going for the win in every category."

My category was Oratorical Interpretation. I loved just saying the words: "oratorical interpretation." Our speech team, like the basketball team, traveled all over the state to compete. For me, a poor kid from a small town, an out-of-town bus trip was positively thrilling. And to compete against a high school in Indianapolis, the state capital, only added to the emotional charge.

It was my first major tournament of my freshman year. We arrived in Indianapolis a little after noon. The high school, a large, imposing building, looked like a fortress. After a quick snack in the cafeteria, the orators were sent to the main auditorium. As the only black person on our team—in fact, as the only black person in the entire tournament—I couldn't help but feel both the pressure and the attention. Both feelings helped fuel my motivation.

*Turn the fear to energy.*

The auditorium, with an overhanging balcony, was mammoth. It was also empty, aside from the judges, who sat in the first row. Built in an architectural era when wood-carved balustrades were all the fashion, the cavernous space looked like it could hold two entire student bodies. A podium had been placed in the center of the stage. The first contestant, a tall lanky boy with a mellifluous voice, was called to recite. He read Lincoln's Gettysburg Address with the polish of a radio announcer. He even looked a little like Lincoln. No doubt about it, he was good.

Next up was a girl who interpreted a speech by Eleanor Roosevelt. She wasn't as strong as the previous contestant, but she was a pretty blonde with a sweet singsong intonation and perfect enunciation. Another potential crowd favorite.

The guy just before me was built like a tank—barrel-chested, with a booming voice that exploded like a cannon. He read Winston Churchill's "blood, sweat, and tears" speech. I knew in an instant he was the one to beat.

"Mr. Smiley," the chief judge finally called, "take your place."

I walked to the podium with measured steps. Then I looked out into the auditorium. Instead of seeing empty seats, I envisioned the great National Mall filled with protestors challenging the government's commitment to the rights of my people. I breathed deeply and thought about the man whose words I was about to read. Then I began:

*I am happy to join with you today in what will go down in history as the greatest demonstration for freedom in the history of our nation.*

*Five score years ago, a great American, in whose sym-*

*bolic shadow we stand today, signed the Emancipation
Proclamation . . .*

As I read, something inside me clicked. Of course, it helped that I had been preparing and practicing for months, that I had memorized the speech verbatim and emulated Dr. King's masterful delivery. I felt the power of his message and the power of the man himself coursing through my veins, feeding my spirit. But I found myself interpreting King according to my own sense of language. I wasn't better than King—no one could hope to achieve that—but I was able to give part of myself to the speech and make it my own.

As the phrases and honeyed words crescendoed and the rhythms quickened, as the metaphors swelled and the emotional resonance of Dr. King's rhetoric rose, I was able to lift the speech to a level I had never reached before. By the time I moved into Dr. King's brilliantly double-ended climax, from his "I have a dream" section to the rich repetitions of his "Let freedom ring" sequence, I knew I had won the judges over.

When I was through, when King's final words rolled off my tongue—"Free at last, free at last; thank God Almighty, we are free at last!"—the judges stood and applauded.

Not only had I won the contest, but more to the point, Dr. King's words had won over the judges' hearts. Just as they had changed the course of a nation, those words would change the course of my life. Ironically, even in the reddest redneck part of the state, these speeches written by perhaps this country's greatest civil-rights activist won the day.

For the next four years I won virtually every speech contest I entered. By channeling Dr. King, I found myself imbued with a steely confidence. I rose to the top of my high school class. I stepped into a leadership role that I dearly relished.

My interests and political awareness outside of school were slowly growing, too. When Ronald Reagan announced his states' rights campaign for the presidency in Philadelphia, Mississippi, the same area where three civil-rights workers—Andrew Goodman, James Earl Chaney, and Michael Henry Schwerner—had been murdered, I understood how calculating his choice of location was.

My parents saw me embracing ideas that were foreign to my strict upbringing. They saw me assuming and asserting greater independence, espousing new views about politics and world events. They saw that they were losing control over me, over the shaping of my mind. As a result, tension in our household escalated.

The lesson I was learning through my extracurricular activities, though, was one I would never forget. As an orator, I was winning not only because my skills were growing but also because my self-image was improving. I was seeing the results of an unshakable truth that motivational experts have known for years: View yourself as a winner, and you become a winner.

# Hustle and Flow

The word *hustle* has several connotations. On the one hand, a hustle is a con move. But *hustle* can also refer to demonstrating extra effort. Cincinnati Reds star Pete Rose was nicknamed Charlie Hustle because of his grit and all-out effort on the field. At Smiley & Sons, my dad's entrepreneurial enterprise, we hustled all the time, cleaning barracks and the base, businesses, and our church. Dad saw an opportunity to bring in extra cash and took advantage of it.

For black America, where survival has always been a daily challenge, hustle takes on particular importance. Someone with good hustle acquires a rhythm of his own, a flow that today we might call being "in the zone."

The flow from my growing ability as an orator was especially sweet. Local newspapers began running articles on my victories. The Kiwanis Club, the American Legion, even the local chamber of commerce invited me to talk at their meetings. By the age of sixteen, I had carved out a speaking circuit based on the powerful messages of the man I considered the leading moral light of the 1960s. At the dawn of the Reagan Revolution, I was getting $50 to $75 an appearance. On the tournament circuit, where victories translated into points to determine the statewide oratory winner at the end of the school year, I was flowing like crazy.

My hustle was in overdrive. Not only was I delivering the speeches of a man I revered above all others, I was getting paid, and I was getting the recognition I craved as a child from a large family living in poverty. When I was elected president of my sophomore class, I was happier than I'd ever been before.

"Where were you last night?" asked Mama.

We had just finished dinner, and I was on my way to my room to study.

"Tournament," I answered blithely with my customary terseness.

"I heard Garnie telling Pam you were in a singing group. Are you in a singing group at school?"

"Yes," I admitted, embarrassed at being found out. "But we don't sing rock 'n' roll. We just sing songs by Barry Manilow, pop songs like 'What the World Needs Now Is Love,' " I explained. In the wake of the beatings, the less my parents knew about my activities, the happier I was.

"So you were telling me a story," Mama said to me. "You weren't at a tournament. You were singing."

I pursed my lips and grimly admitted it.

"I'm gonna have to talk to your daddy about this. You join a singing group without our permission, and then you make up a story about it."

"I'm sorry," I said. "But the school singing group is no big deal. The school loans us tuxes, and we perform at different functions and events."

"Dances?"

"They aren't dances," I explained. "We give concerts."

"Do the singers dance?"

"We do some steps. But we aren't dancing with each other, and the audience isn't dancing."

"And you say it's no big deal to make up some story."

I started to say something sharp in response, but held my tongue. Nothing I could have said would have made any difference. Mama stomped off to her bedroom to discuss the matter with Daddy.

After my hospitalization, my parents were careful not to beat me. Mama and Daddy understood that beating was off limits because of what had happened, though I doubt they were happy about it. I, in turn, continued to punish them by contemptuously tossing off yes or no answers to their questions about my schedule, tournaments, and friends. My silent treatment angered them deeply, but there was nothing they could do. Without the use of corporeal punishment, they were stalemated. I figured there was nothing they could do to hurt me. Man, was I wrong!

"I talked to your father," Mama said a few minutes later, emerging from their bedroom. "We decided that you won't be able to compete in another speech tournament for the next three weeks."

"*What!*" I exclaimed, furious.

"You heard me, Tavis."

"That's not fair," I protested. "I'll miss two tournaments. That's two chances for first-place ribbons. Each ribbon means ten points. Without those points I might not win all-state."

"Discussion over," Mama said.

I started to reply angrily, but held my tongue again.

Looking back, I can see that my mother and father had to find a new way of punishing me. Since whippings were no longer feasible, their options were limited. They couldn't take away my allowance; I didn't have any. They couldn't take away permission to drive the family car for the same reason: I had no such permission. My only real asset was my intellectual currency. Believing in the necessity of discipline, they decided to restrict my extracurricular academic pursuits. That's what I lived for—and where I was most vulnerable.

I didn't react well to their efforts to rein me in. Rather than placate or engage them, I became even more withdrawn at home. I employed silence with greater frequency and for longer spells. I always did what they asked; I fulfilled my many obligations at church, did my homework, and worked in the evenings and weekends at Dad's cleaning operation. But I refused to give them any of myself. My spirit remained walled off. I resisted them as fiercely as if I were Gandhi defying the British Empire. Even Big Mama, whom I loved dearly, couldn't convince me to behave otherwise.

Big Mama and I sat at the kitchen table. My parents weren't home, and my siblings were outside playing. Having Big Mama to myself was always a treat. When she was in a talkative mood, I'd stop whatever I was doing to listen. She'd fix me some hot cocoa and settle back to tell her stories. When she spoke, she spoke in the slow seductive cadences of the Deep South. And on this particular autumn day, she had a special story she wanted to tell me.

"This here happened some time back, Tavis. Happened when I was working for a white lady in Gulfport whose husband was a rich lawyer. Lady's name was Petunia—always thought that was a strange name—and her husband was Mortimer. I called him Mr. Mort for short, and he liked that. He was a friendly man, yes he was, with a smile for everyone, including your Big Mama. I'd been working at the home of his friend, Mr. Thomas Alvison, but Mr. Alvison upped and moved to Atlanta. When Mr. Alvison recommended me to Mr. Mort, Mr. Mort said, 'Well, sure, 'cause the cleaning lady we have now must be going blind 'cause she don't see the dust and dirt hiding under the carpet and all up on the bookshelves.' Well, I don't have to tell you, Tavis, how your Big Mama hates dust and dirt. I go after dust and dirt like a hound after a rabbit. Problem was, Mrs. Petunia liked her other cleaning lady and didn't want to let her go. Mr. Mort insisted and, sure enough, I was hired. Now, back in those days a wife couldn't tell a husband who to hire or fire, so Mrs. Petunia was stuck with me. And she didn't like me one bit. Now that's all right. Folk don't have to like you. Not everybody will and not everybody should. I can live without folk liking me 'cause the good Lord does more than like me; the good Lord loves me. But Mrs. Petunia wasn't showing me no love. Whenever I'd ask if my work was to her satisfaction—did she like the way I polished the silver? Did I wax up the dining-room floor to a bright enough shine?—she whispered something so low I couldn't hear her. When I asked her to repeat herself, she'd just leave the room. She acted like my questions didn't even deserve an answer. I wasn't good enough to *get* an answer. Finally I said something to Mr. Mort, 'cause I don't like being where I am not wanted. 'Mr. Mort,' I said, 'your wife is not happy with my work.'

" 'Nonsense,' he told me. 'You're a good worker.'

" 'Well, sir, when I ask her if everything's all right, she don't even answer me.'

" 'I'm sure everything's all right,' he said. 'You just go on with your work.'

"I tried to go on, and, in fact, I worked there quite a spell longer. But truth be told, Tavis, that lady's attitude got to me. She had poisoned the atmosphere for me by going around and never saying nothing to me. It was meaner than if she had up and cussed me out. That's how she drove me away from her, without saying a word. Funny part is, when your Paw Paw asked me what did Mrs. Petunia say to make me quit, I had to say, 'Nothing.' "

Big Mama stopped her story, took my hand, and slipped me a ten-dollar bill. Big Mama loved giving me extra money.

"Now you go buy something for yourself," she said. "You treat yourself. And mind me, son, watch how you treat your mama and daddy. They don't deserve no disrespect."

"Yes, ma'am," I replied.

I heard Big Mama's gentle chastisement. But when it came to Mama and Daddy, my heart was still dark. I hadn't found my way to forgive and forget.

On another day, I was outside the trailer talking to a schoolmate. We were arguing about what the number-one song was on the hit parade, Michael Jackson's "Rock with You" or the Captain and Tennille's "Do That to Me One More Time." I was a Michael fan and knew that his song was in the top slot. My friend said otherwise. I argued strenuously, citing evidence of a radio-show countdown that I had just heard, telling my pal that he had no idea what he was talking about. Big Mama overheard the exchange and afterward called me to her room.

"Tavis," she said, "there's no harm in disagreeing with someone else, son. But it's *how* you disagree that matters."

"What do you mean, Big Mama?"

"There are folk who argue to make their point, and there are folk who argue to make someone else feel bad."

"Well, you should feel bad if you're wrong."

"You should feel good if someone is setting you right," she corrected me. "The idea of disagreeing is to help the person who got the information wrong, not to beat up on him. The idea is to help, not hurt. Now you think about that next time you go off on your friends with that sharp mouth of yours, you understand?"

"Yes, ma'am."


I can still hear Big Mama's words echoing inside me, still feel Big Mama's love. She was all about tolerance and understanding. And even though I couldn't always act on her lessons of patience and love at the time she gave them to me, her wisdom remains in me to this day. She taught me how important it is for young people to honor the older generation. I was lucky to have her as a fount of spiritual truth. I'm constantly encouraging young people to develop nurturing relationships with their grandparents and vice versa. If we don't have grandparents, we can look for older surrogates or mentors eager to step into the role. The young and old need each other. Together, they can make sense of the world. They can bridge the gap of misunderstanding and provide each other with what they need—attention, love, and respect.

# Dangerous Unselfishness

The second great speech by Dr. Martin Luther King Jr. that I presented in competition was the one he delivered in Memphis, Tennessee, on April 3, 1968, the eve of his assassination. It was the address in which he foresaw his own death and yet declared, like the Savior who informed his heart, that he was not "fearing any man." He had been to the mountaintop. He had earned a glimpse of glory. In doing so, he urged us to develop a quality that granted him greatness even as that very quality agitated his enemies. He called that quality "dangerous unselfishness" and cited an incident in the life of Christ to illustrate his point.

To King, unselfishness involved turning the "I" in our lives to "thou," focusing not on ourselves but on our sisters and brothers. Later in life, I'd hear Dr. Cornel West use different words to make a similar point: "You can't lead the people," declared Dr. West, "if you don't love the people. And you can't save the people, if you don't serve the people."

While I was working in the office of Councilman Hogan, the

concept of service became my passion. To me, Hogan was the loving epistle of what I was reading in King. King said that life's most persistent and urgent question is, *What are you doing for others?* Well, all Councilman Hogan did *was* serve others. King said that to serve others takes a heart full of grace and a soul generated by love. Hogan had that heart and had that soul. More than Hank Aaron or Michael Jackson or Muhammad Ali, Hogan became my hero. Dr. King tells us that any of us can be great because any of us can serve. But it was Hogan who got me hooked on the nobility of public service. Even today, that is why I do what I do: to serve.

Mom and Dad wanted my universe defined and determined by the church. To them, church was the sum and substance of what makes life and the afterlife worthwhile. They saw the Holiness church saving our family from the temptations of the material world. Nothing would have pleased Mama more than if I had decided to become a Holiness preacher. Life inside church was simple: the rules were laid out, salvation was spelled out, the laws of God and theology were absolute. Life outside church, however, was anything *but* simple: moral relativism ran rampant, values were upended, moral confusion and sin seemed to trump sense. Our worldview within the church excluded multiculturalism; the wider world encouraged it.

One thing I've found in life is that God, as I understand God, shows up where you least expect him. I believe God showed up in my teenage years in the person of Councilman Hogan. God made sure that the councilman attended Elder Mills's church, and God made sure that Councilman Hogan connected with me. Our connection was so tight and right that, at age sixteen, I was able to engage politically on a level with people twice my age. As a result of that engagement, I was invited by him to a fund-raiser for the Democratic Party.

"Tavis," said the councilman, "I want you to go as my guest. There's someone I want you to meet."

I walked into the Hyatt Regency Hotel in Indianapolis feeling decidedly underdressed. My lone blue suit was a little shiny, my white shirt was frayed at the collar, my red tie had seen better days, and my black wing tip shoes needed new soles. But I put my feelings of insecurity aside and walked into the hotel like I belonged there. And in the course of a long evening, I discovered that I did belong. More amazingly, I discovered I belonged to a universe far larger than any I had ever imagined.

Councilman Hogan directed me to the dais where our places were reserved. I saw my name printed on a card in front of my seat: "Mr. Tavis Smiley, Assistant to the Councilman." It was the first time in my life I'd been addressed as "Mr." The card to my right indicated Hogan's place. And when I looked down at the card to my left, I couldn't believe my eyes. It read "Senator Birch Bayh." Birch Bayh was Indiana's senior U.S. senator, the most prominent politician in Indiana, a national figure. He'd served in the Indiana House of Representatives as minority leader and speaker. In the U.S. Senate, he had risen to prominence as a member of the Select Committee on Intelligence. In a state marked by conservatism—after all, Indiana had once housed the headquarters of the Ku Klux Klan—Bayh had valiantly campaigned as a committed liberal. And I was seated next to him!

Could the seating arrangement be a mistake? I wondered. Suddenly I became aware of a buzz at the back of the room as the doors opened and the senator and members of his staff entered. The crowd rose to applaud him. It took the senator ten minutes to make his way to the dais. Everyone seemed to want to shake his hand and exchange a few words. Bayh effortlessly accommodated his well-wishers. I studied him carefully from the dais. He focused intently on whomever he was speaking to, looking them in the eye, his manner friendly and forthright. When he reached the dais, he and Councilman Hogan embraced. I was impressed that Councilman Hogan and Senator Bayh were so well acquainted. Then Hogan introduced me, calling me "a bright young man with a keen interest in politics." The senator looked at me, shook my hand, and said, "Great meeting you, Tavis. Glad we can break bread together."

At last, Senator Bayh took his seat. A prayer followed welcoming remarks by the local Democratic Party chairman. As dinner was served, a long stream of people made their way to the dais to say hello to the senator. He seemed to know everyone by name and showed no irritation at having his dinner constantly interrupted. At a certain point, the people stopped approaching and focused on their dinners; to my delight, Senator Bayh turned his attention to me. He was a handsome man with an easy smile. In his early fifties, the senator looked even younger. His dark pin-striped suit and light blue tie gave him an ambassadorial demeanor. When he began questioning me, I suppose I could have been intimidated and clammed up. Instead, I found the wherewithal to engage him in conversation. It was, without doubt, a turning point in my life.

I mentioned that I was president of my class and discussed my success on the oratorical interpretation circuit. That led us into a discussion of Martin Luther King Jr. Because I had devoured so many books on King's life and knew his speeches so well, I was not the least bit shy about discussing King. The senator asked if I was familiar with King's letter from the Birmingham City Jail. I told him I was, and we talked about Dr. King's four prescribed steps in a nonviolent campaign (citing the injustices, negotiation, self-purification, direct action). He asked if I remembered how King replied to accusations that he was an extremist. I replied that King had seen it as a compliment, that he cited Amos as an extremist for justice, Paul as an extremist for the gospel of Jesus, and Christ himself as an extremist in his evocation of love.

"You know Dr. King's writings, Tavis," the senator said.

"To me, his language reads like music," I said.

"The great orators," said the senator, "are all musical. It's the music in their language that lifts their ideas to an even higher level."

Before long, we were discussing Abraham Lincoln and Winston Churchill. The senator was curious about the speech competition and about the ethnic constituency of my high school. He was fascinated by the fact that I was one of the few black kids in my school district. He asked if that posed any difficulty for me. I told him, if anything, it presented even greater motivation; I wanted to represent my race with distinction.

The senator went on to talk about the importance of representing the average man, the little guy. I lit up inside when he discussed the nobility of public service. I, too, wanted to serve. I, too, wanted to grow up to become a United States senator. I wanted to spend my days exchanging ideas with men like Birch Bayh.

And so our conversation went, back and forth—this conversation between a famous politician and a high school kid. It was nothing short of amazing to me that I was able to hold such a lively dialogue with such a learned man.

The lesson was clear: I didn't have to be intimidated by anyone. Intimidation comes from lack of confidence, and lack of confidence comes from low self-esteem. Think well of yourself and no one will intimidate you. Besides, important men like Birch Bayh speak to people not to show off their importance but to engage others on a human level. Great people don't intimidate. They make you feel welcome and worthwhile.

*If I can hold my own with Senator Birch Bayh*, I silently told myself, *I can talk to anyone.*

"Watch how you talk to me," my mother said.

It was shortly after I had joined the high school speech team when Mama asked me how often the team would meet. I replied, "What difference does it make to you?"

"It makes a difference," said Mama, "because it means more preparation and after-school activities. I think you've taken on too much, Tavis."

"No, I haven't."

"Look what you're doing. You're in the singing group, you go to the speech contests, now the debate team, not to mention the student council."

"I'm managing them."

"I'm not sure."

"Well, I am," I said adamantly. After all, I wasn't in any organized after-school sports and my grades were high.

"Watch that mouth of yours, boy."

"I know what I'm doing, Mama."

"You think you know what you're doing, Tavis. You think you know everything." Mama's instinct had always been to hold me back, to restrain the eagerness and energy with which I longed to engage the world. Looking back, I'm sure she was just being protective of me, concerned that I would take on too much and falter. But at the time I felt her smothering me.

"And now you've been elected president of next year's junior class. You need to give up one of these things."

"I'm not giving up anything."

"You are if I say you are."

"This is my business, Mama, not yours."

"You're over the line, boy. You're asking for it."

"What are you going to do?" I asked angrily. "Have Dad get out the extension cord?"

Bristling at my defiance, Mama snapped back, "I'm having you resign from being president of the junior class, that's what I'm going to do."

"You can't do that."

"Watch me."

"I campaigned for months. I worked night and day. Do you know what a big honor it is? No one resigns after winning the election. It's crazy. It doesn't make any sense."

"What doesn't make any sense is you taking on all this extra stuff at school."

"You can't force me to quit."

"Boy, I don't have to force you. I'll go over there to that school myself and tell them you're resigning."

"You wouldn't dare."

"You're wrong."

And just like that, Mama marched over to the school and told the principal that I had to give up the presidency.

I was incredulous. And I was furious. It was unprecedented for a class president to quit; there was no mechanism to replace me. Would the school even honor my resignation? I'd already been sophomore class president. The junior presidency was a far more important position; it was the junior class president who planned the senior prom, the social event of everyone's high school career. It would be the ultimate test of my organizational abilities, a test I intended to pass with flying colors.

Mama had to understand what an honor it was to win this office. She had to be stopped. Didn't she understand that my resignation would be yet another public humiliation for me?

Mama couldn't do this! But she did do it. Mama told the principal, "Tavis cannot be president of the junior class. He's taken on too much. With his church responsibilities and his speech tournaments, he's already running around like a chicken with his head cut off."

"I hope you'll reconsider, Mrs. Smiley," the principal said.

"My husband and I have talked about it," she said, "and this is our final decision."

Before long, the whole school found out that Mama had made me resign the presidency. I was thoroughly humiliated. And this second act of humiliation was totally uncalled for. It was just their way of getting back at me for being too independent. I knew I could never forgive them. If I was angry at them before, my anger now turned to rage.

Looking back, I realize that there was a tremendous lesson to be learned here. None of this had to play out the way it did. Had I been able to hear the concern in my mama's voice and bridge the distance between our positions, I might not have pushed her to restrict my extracurricular activities so drastically. But by hardening my position, by closing all genuine effort to treat her concerns with respect, I forced her to harden her position. In the end, we both lost out.

# Conflict of Sufferings

Soon I found my own vehicle of retaliation.

"Since you feel I've taken on too much," I told Mama one evening shortly after she had forced me to resign the class presidency, "I'm quitting the church choir."

"Over my dead body. You're the junior choir director."

"Not anymore."

"The other kids depend on you."

"The other kids will do fine without me."

"I'm not having this, Tavis."

"You were the one who said I was doing too much."

"Doing too much *school*," said Mama. "You can't do too much church. How can you do too much for God?"

"I'm not sure God cares whether or not I sing in the choir."

"You're singing in that choir—and that's it."

"I've already quit. I told Elder Mills yesterday. I resigned, just the way you resigned my presidency of the junior class."

"Well then, *un*resign."

"It's too late. Elder Mills already appointed someone else."

"Fine, you go on and quit the choir. You go on and see how far this hardheadedness of yours is going to get you. I'm going to talk to your father about this."

As dinner finished that night, silence hung in the air. I refused to say a word to Mama, and she wasn't talking to me. My brothers were their usual rambunctious selves, oblivious to the standoff in front of them. From his place at the head of the table, Daddy chastised the boys when they got too unruly and, once everyone was finished eating, instructed us to finish our homework before we headed out to the base to clean up the mess hall. As I got up to leave the table, he stopped me.

"Hold on, Tabo," he said. "We gotta talk."

Sensing a thunderstorm, my siblings hurried away.

"Your mother told me you quit choir without our permission."

"Yes, sir," I replied, wanting to keep this conversation short.

"She said that was your way of getting back at her. Is she right?"

"You'll have to ask her."

"I'm asking you, son."

"I don't know."

"Well, if you don't know, who does?"

"I don't know."

"Is that all you have to say?"

"Yes, sir."

"Then here's what I have to say. You won't be allowed to enter the next two speech tournaments."

"Is Mama's making you say this?"

"Your mother and I are a united front. We do what's best for our kids, and we do it together. We can't have you rebelling against us or against our wishes. It's just not going to happen, Tavis."

"Whatever," I said darkly, knowing that there was no way to win this argument.

Looking back at the antagonism between me and my parents, I'm still amazed how my relationship with God endured. Others might think that my anger would have infected my relationship with him. But from my earliest days, I had been taught the miracle of God's grace. That grace overwhelmed the small injustices of the church, its pastor, and my parents. That grace sustained my spirit in ways that I may not have been able to express at the time, but it reined in any destructive behavior.

I still found Sunday school absorbing. The Bible, in all its wondrous complexity and with its richly narrated stories, remained a book that excited my imagination. The language of the King James translation stirred my soul, just as it had Dr. King's. I knew it contained a wealth of timeless truths and wisdom. To grasp the lessons of its parables and the meaning of its symbolism required ongoing study. I welcomed that study. From my vantage point, the chief challenges for me were: How am I to understand God? and, How is the Bible to help me in that understanding?

I recall one Sunday when I was asked to lead our Sunday school class. This wasn't an uncommon occurrence. Our teacher, recognizing my intellectual curiosity, encouraged me to speak out. She saw that I had a knack for explaining difficult passages. This Sunday's explanation involved the letter to the Hebrews.

I knew what the commentaries said, that this epistle contained perhaps the most profound apostolic expressions in the entire Bible. One famous writer called this letter "the sum of the gospel."

This was heady stuff. As I read through Hebrews, I stopped at chapter 10, verse 32, and recited the words "conflict of sufferings." Certainly the poetry of the phrase struck me. But there was something else that hit home. The writer was talking to the Jews about the hard times they faced after being baptized in the name of Jesus. But "conflict of sufferings" brought to mind what I was going through with my parents, what many kids went through. My parents opposed my participation in debate tournaments and speech contests. They resisted many of my attempts to reach out to the larger world. But I also knew my mother and father loved me deeply. Daddy was the hardest working man in the world, and he did it all for the welfare of our family. My mother was a pillar of strength and devotion. I may not have been able to express my feelings about these conflicting emotions—my anger and love, my resentment and gratitude—but I knew they resulted in their own kind of suffering.

At the beginning of the next section in Hebrews—chapter 11— I discovered a Scripture of such power that, to this day, it resonates with particular urgency. "Faith is the substance of things hoped for, and the evidence of things not seen." We had just been studying the concept of paradox in English—and I immediately saw its application in Hebrews.

In that moment I realized that *I* had faith. There was so much I hoped for—a future of achievement, a world beyond rural Indiana, a life filled with excitement and challenge. And the fact that "the invisible is often more real than the visible," as one commentator put it, added to that excitement. In other words, I saw that faith is built on a mystery. Faith is built on hope. Faith can never be destroyed because faith is not material. Faith is spiritual, and the spirit ultimately defeats all fear.

In explaining this concept of faith to my classmates, I didn't have the words I'm using now. But I did have a gut-level understanding that I was dealing with an article of absolute conviction.

When our Sunday school teacher asked me to tell the class what Hebrews 11:1 meant to me, I was quick to say, "You don't have to see it to believe it."

The next Sunday, another sister in the church, who knew of my interest in poetry and rhetoric, arranged with Elder Mills to have me perform a literary work in front of the full congregation. I chose "The Creation," a poem written in the early 1920s by the African American writer James Weldon Johnson. I chose it not only because its theological underpinnings were compatible with our Pentecostal church but because of its dramatic language.

At the designated point in the service, I went to the pulpit, stood in the preacher's place and began speaking to the congregation.

*And God stepped out on space,*
*And He looked around said,*
"I'm lonely—
I'll make me a world."

The poem is a narrative paraphrasing Genesis in a folksy but eloquent patois. I loved the theatricality of its vernacular. It gave me a chance to demonstrate my oratorical prowess. Standing in the pulpit where our pastor had lashed out against Phyllis and me years before, it was my time to shine, to show our church what I had learned about public speaking and the role of language in stirring the heart. I pushed Johnson's poetic language to its limits, and then some. When I got through, it felt as though the world, through Johnson's imagery, was created anew. The church exploded with applause. Everyone was on their feet. And when I looked down at the second pew, the private domain of the Smiley family, I saw my siblings cheering, and much to my delight, so were my folks. I felt good about having done something at church that pleased my parents. It was a welcome respite from the emotional warfare that marked our daily lives.

Did that signal that a truce had been declared between us?

Unfortunately, it didn't. The worst part of our struggles had just begun.

# The Paradox Paradigm

I was in it, but I didn't know it. I was constructing it, living it, without the slightest idea of what I was doing.

I give it a fancy name now. I call it the Paradox Paradigm. That's certainly not a name I would have used or understood then. In retrospect I can see how I compartmentalized my life. To a great degree, it's still something I do. That may be both a gift and a burden. However I view it, it was the Paradox Paradigm that got me through.

## Paradox 1

Although I was the most talkative guy at school, at home I still never said a word to my parents. The push-pull between us—their keeping me out of more and more school activities, my getting *into* more and more school activities—reached an endpoint. I wouldn't give and neither would they.

**Paradox 2**

The brooding and silent Tavis at home, playing the part of an extreme introvert, transformed himself into an extreme extrovert at school. Senior year was when I hit my stride. After the indignity of having to resign the junior-class presidency, I bounced back with a vengeance. To spite my parents and delight my overactive ego, I campaigned vigorously and victoriously for the office of president of the senior class.

**Paradox 3**

Tavis the extreme extrovert—who was voted most likely to succeed and was the speech-team captain and yearbook editor—never had a single girlfriend in high school.

It wasn't that I lacked raging hormones—my hormones raged with the best of them—but rather that I adhered to the codified behavior proscribed by the New Bethel Tabernacle Church. At age seventeen, I still had not been to a movie theater, still had never tasted an alcoholic beverage or a drug (that's still true to this day), still had not been intimate with a girl.

In the white world of Maconaquah High, I was close to many girls—some were my best friends—but because the relationships were platonic, I avoided the distractions of romantic drama. I could concentrate on senior-class business.

**Paradox 4**

Although my connection to Councilman Hogan had solidified my growing liberalism, my most meaningful dialogues this final year of high school took place with Mr. Beall, my government teacher who was a white conservative Republican. I loved Mr. Beall. He engaged me in some of the most spirited conversations of my young life. Exceedingly sharp himself, he sharpened my own polemical skills. We not only argued politics, we went nose to nose on theology. I was still espousing the Pentecostal principles while Mr. Beall's Christianity took a decidedly Baptist turn. Delineating the nuances of doctrine was a fine exercise in mental stamina. I loved the banter because the banter was loving—God and government seen from opposing points of view. Mr. Beall egged me on, but he did so with a twinkle in his eye. Instead of getting vicious, the disputes became a training ground in supporting my ability to reason.

Another paradox: Even though the arguments were personal— I personally believed in a greater government role in aiding the disenfranchised—Mr. Beall had a way of depersonalizing the emotional dynamics. It wasn't as important to be right as it was to be cogent in presenting your case. Mr. Beall mentored me in the art of intellectual exchange rendered with erudition and charm.


Yet that charm completely eluded me at home. The closer I came to graduating, the more distant my parents became. Those times at church when I won over the congregation by reciting a poem or a speech by Dr. King were not enough to change things.

Of course, I get it now in a way I couldn't have gotten it then. As high school wound down, my parents saw that they were losing me—perhaps forever. They saw that, given my ambition to go to college and beyond, they were on the verge of watching their first son enter a world they had worked so exhaustively to circumvent, to protect me against. Soon all their restrictions and rules would fall, and I'd be gone, free to do, think, and act as I pleased.

I now know that fear was what kept my folks from filling out any college forms for me. They adamantly refused. The prospect of my going to college only heightened their hostility.

My frustration grew. It was late in my senior year, and I had all the forms for Indiana University spread across the kitchen table. I needed Mama and Dad to complete the financial aid papers.

"Not now," said Dad.

"You keep saying 'not now,' " I said, "but the deadline's about to pass. You have to answer these questions tonight."

I read my parents the queries out loud.

"We don't know how to answer these questions," said Mama.

"Well, if you don't, who does?" I asked.

"You're the smart one," said Dad. "You've always got the answer. *You* answer the questions."

"I can't. They have to do with you and your income."

"We don't intend to put our business out there," said Mama.

I threw up my hands and filled out the forms as best I could. I ignored the financial aid addendum and left half the other questions blank. I mailed it off without my parents' signatures. They flat refused to sign.

A month later a letter addressed to me arrived in the mail.

I was accepted to Indiana University.

Come hell or high water, I was going to college.


The memory of my beating still loomed large in my mind. I was still trying to get past it, to prove my worth and overcome my shame with oversized achievement.

Looking back on it, I realize that the beating and its aftermath both softened me and toughened me—softened me so that I came to empathize with others, toughened me to get through whatever came my way. The incident forced me to see beyond present pain and look to God for direction.

Everything that happened to me in high school convinced me I had certain God-given gifts, and the gifts were given to me for a reason. No one could dissuade me from that truth. That truth brought me to the gates of Indiana University and fortified my resolve to get an education, no matter what.

# IU

I went off to Indiana University with nothing more than $50 in my pocket and a small suitcase.

A friend, Councilman Hogan's son Danny, drove me to Bloomington. I gave him half my money for gas for the two-and-a-half-hour drive. As we headed down the state, I was both excited and nervous. It was a day of firsts. I was leaving home for the first time. I was the first in my family to step into the world of higher education. And for the first time I would be living on my own, without restrictions, without rules, without the nightly church meetings and our cleaning work for Smiley & Sons.

I had excelled in high school, but would I measure up in college? I had no idea what to expect. Going without my parents' approval or help didn't make matters any easier. I had no dorm assignment, no money for tuition, no financial aid. I had nothing but my letter of acceptance.

"What are you going to do when you get there?" my brother Garnie had asked when the family had gathered outside the house.

Our family had moved from the trailer to a house in Kokomo that my parents had bought from the estate of deceased members of New Bethel Tabernacle Church.

"I'm not sure," I said. "But I'll figure it out."

"You scared to be going so far from home?" asked my brother Maury.

"I'll miss you guys, sure," I said. "But you'll come visit me. You'll come down to Bloomington."

As my siblings all gathered around to hug me, I saw Mama and Dad looking on. Then Dad stepped forward and shook my hand.

"You'll do fine, Tabo," he said. "God gave you a good mind."

When Mama slowly approached me, I saw tears in her eyes. We didn't know what to say to each other. Finally she hugged me with all her might and simply said, "Oh, Tavis. I love you so much."

Tears came to my eyes. I didn't want to break down with my siblings all around, so I broke away, saying, "I love you too."


The campus was enormous, a lot bigger in size than the town of Bunker Hill. The university population, perhaps thirty-two thousand strong, was on par with the city of Kokomo. The sprawling landscape of buildings—science labs, athletic fields, auditoriums, chapels, dormitories—was overwhelming.

Standing there in front of a dormitory on the campus of Indiana University, holding my little suitcase and my letter, I felt like a country hick.

Where was my place in all this?

All I knew was that I was standing in front of a dorm that housed students, and I needed a place to put down my suitcase. I walked into a front lobby filled with boxes and suitcases. Young men and women accompanied by their parents streamed in and out carrying portable stereos and boxes of books and bedspreads. I looked at a large piece of paper pinned to the bulletin board listing room assignments. I looked for my name. Of course, it wasn't there. As far as Indiana University knew, I didn't exist. I had never returned the form accepting admission because my parents had never signed it.

With a combination of naiveté and determination, I had simply shown up.

I could have lost it and gone running back to Kokomo. I could have let the feeling of intimidation turn me right around. I could have shrunk within myself and given in to feelings of isolation and fear.

*Turn the fear to energy.*

And that's what I did. I turned my apprehension into action. The action involved taking one step at a time. To begin with, I needed to find a place to put down my suitcase and sleep for the night. It was after 6 P.M. and the administration offices were closed. No one was going to give me a room tonight. At the end of the hallway, though, I saw a small sitting area with an easy chair and a couch. No one was using the space. Nor were there any signs declaring the area off limits. So I put down my suitcase on the couch and silently claimed the space as my own. I sat there for a long while, thinking how amazing it was to be in college, with no idea how any of this was going to work out.

One step at a time.

Next, I went down to the dorm cafeteria. Fortunately, no one was taking names or asking for food passes. First-day chaos allowed me to move through the line and get a free meal.

Families were gathered together. Old friends, reunited after the summer, excitedly discussed what they had done and where they had been. I sat alone, not really feeling sorry for myself, but feeling anonymous. And in fact, I was anonymous. And that feeling was new. After all, for the past four years I'd been a big shot at Maconaquah High School. I knew everyone and everyone knew me. People respected my accomplishments, and I reveled in that recognition. My place in that universe was secure. Here I had no place—not now, maybe not ever.

After dinner I went back to the public area of the dorm, sat on the couch, and read the *Indiana Daily Student,* a college newspaper more sophisticated than the *Kokomo Tribune.* I was surprised at the diversity of articles, movie reviews, music reviews, and editorials. I was amazed at the variety of activities on campus. Once I was through with the paper, though, I had nothing to do. It was only nine o'clock, too early to go to sleep. With the assistance of their parents, students were still moving in, carrying lamps and trunks, tennis rackets and cartons of clothes. I noticed how helpful the other parents were. I couldn't help but feel the advantages of family bonds at such a critical time in the students' lives. Right around now, my brothers would be getting home from church.

By eleven, the noise had died down. I could have used the bathroom down the hall and changed into my pajamas, but that would have made me even more conspicuous. I decided just to stretch out on the couch and sleep in my clothes. Chances were, no one would notice. And no one did. I drifted off, my overstimulated mind scrambled with thoughts. My dreams were a wild surreal movie, with tornadoes roaring through cornfields and demolishing trailer parks in their wake. I was in a version of *The Wizard of Oz* set in Indiana. Senator Bayh was in the dream and so was Elder Rufus Mills, who was the Wizard. Dr. King worked as a professor at Indiana University, where he welcomed me to his class. The fictitious boxcar children figured into the dream—I don't remember exactly how—and all the Smiley children were under my protection as we huddled together in the dark woods.

When morning broke, I didn't know where I was. Then I remembered—on a couch in a dorm in Bloomington, Indiana. I yawned and stretched.

"Don't you have a room?" asked a student who noticed me.

"Not yet," I said.

He just nodded and moved on.

I needed to eat and, once again, was able to join the cafeteria line and treat myself to a free breakfast. I picked up the local paper, the *Bloomington Herald-Times*, and scanned the news: Reagan at an economic summit, Princess Grace of Monaco had been killed in a horrific car wreck on the Riviera. It all seemed so far away. The *Indiana Daily Student* was filled with articles on how and where to register for classes; the information went over my head.

I knew one thing: I had to find the admissions office.

A pretty coed told me where it was, and I was off.

"May I help you?" asked the first secretary I encountered.

I told her my story.

"I'm not sure what to tell you," she said quizzically. So she sent me to a second secretary. Again, I told my story. Again, the secretary was confused.

"I've never heard of a case like yours," she said. "I'm not sure you belong here."

"Oh, I belong here," I replied. "I have this letter that says so."

"But the letter's not enough. You need proof of tuition payment, a room assignment, and any number of other documents. You can't just waltz in here and go to college."

"I *have* to go to college," I said. "I *am* going to college."

The process went on and on. I moved from one secretary to another. Finally, nearly three hours after I had arrived, I found myself sitting across the desk from the director of admissions, a white man in his fifties. He, too, had a puzzled look on his face.

"We've called the bursar's office, Mr. Smiley," he said, "but they have no information on you. You're nowhere to be found in their records. You never applied for aid, and you never sent in payment for tuition."

"I know," I said.

"In fact, there's no real reason you should be here."

"I understand, sir, except I do have my letter of admission."

"I've looked up your high school record, Mr. Smiley, and it's outstanding. That's why you were admitted. But you never wrote us back to say you were coming."

I explained that was because of my parents' refusal to sign any of the forms.

The director scratched his head. "Mr. Smiley," he said, "I'm going to send you to see David Hummons, our associate bursar. I'm hoping David can help you."

Much to my amazement, David Hummons was a tall, barrel-chested black man with a full-blown Afro and a laid-back attitude.

"What's happening, brother?" he asked me as we crowded into his cubicle.

I didn't know whether to call him "brother" or "sir." In high school, I didn't have a single black teacher or administrator. This was new territory. To me, David Hummons looked like someone out of the movie *Superfly*.

"Man," he said, "how you gonna go to this school—you got no room assignment and you got no money. I bet you don't even have the funds to pay for your books."

"No, sir, I don't."

"Brother, you are one raggedy Negro. You just show up here hoping this university will take you in. Is that it?"

"Yes, sir."

Hummons laughed so loudly a secretary came in to see what was so funny. The laugh, though, wasn't mean; it was a warm and engaging laugh, almost a laugh of appreciation.

"Tell you what, young Tavis Smiley, I have no notion how all this will work out, but I do have a friend who might have an idea or two."

Hummons picked up the phone, dialed a number, and said, "Jimmy, I have a young man here with the strange name of Tavis. You won't believe his story. I'll let him tell it to you, but the bottom line is that he just showed up as a freshman with nothing but a toothbrush and a smile. The smile ain't all that pretty, but something tells me this kid's all right. Can I send him up?"

Five minutes later I was waiting outside the office of Jimmy Ross, director of financial aid. I waited for nearly an hour.

"Mr. Ross will see you now," the secretary finally announced.

Sitting behind a big desk in a big office was, much to my unspoken delight, another black man. Jimmy Ross was also a brother!

Jimmy Ross totally understood my story. He understood the Pentecostal church and its resistance to the outside world. I didn't have to explain.

"What you will have to do," said Ross, "is fill out a million forms. We're going to straighten you out, Brother Smiley, but it's going to take a mountain of paperwork to do it."

And so I began to climb that mountain. I filled out forms till my fingers practically fell off. I filled out admissions forms, financial forms, forms for student employment and forms for Pell Grants. At the end of the day, when the forms were completed and

I took them into Ross's office, he and David Hummons were standing together in the middle of a conversation. They both turned to me with broad beautiful smiles on their faces.

"Welcome to IU," said Ross.

"Make us proud, young brother," added Hummons, slapping me on the back.

"I will, sir," I promised solemnly. "You know I will."

It's a lesson I'll never forget. No one in this life gets ahead without the help of a lot of other people. Even the most talented need others to point out the way or lend a hand. Without Councilman Hogan and so many others, I never would have made my way to IU. Without the help of David Hummons and Jimmy Ross, my career at IU would have been over before it started. Anyone who thinks he's gotten ahead in life without the help of others is living in a fool's paradise.

## Brave New World

I was assigned a room at Read Hall, the only dorm with private bathrooms. Read sat atop a hill with a commanding view of the campus. Everyone called it the best dorm at IU. I was sitting pretty; the brothers had hooked me up.

My roommate was a white farmboy named Chris, and he and I got along well. I'd grown up with lots of guys just like him in high school, guys who had elected me class president three times.

I went through registration, signing up for the core courses. My financial-aid package included a Pell Grant and a work-study program that put me back in the bursar's office working with David Hummons. My job—talk about irony—was to call the parents of students who owed tuition money. I was given the job because of what Hummons called my "authoritative voice." Actually, I liked the work because, given my background, I sympathized with people having financial trouble and gave them a break whenever I could. I had a knack for gently but firmly suggesting easy payment plans. The job carried considerable responsibility, and shouldering that responsibility helped me feel like I belonged at IU.

Off campus, I faced a new battery of challenges. I could now go to parties and stay out all night. But that didn't interest me. I could go to bars and drink my uncertainties away. But that idea repelled me. Yet hanging out with people from different cultures and backgrounds interested me enormously.

My interest in African American culture found new expression on almost every level. IU was made up of black students from Chicago, Detroit, and even New York. They had an urban hipness and edgy attitude far different from what I had experienced in rural Indiana. They talked differently, walked differently, and viewed the world with eyes far more experienced than mine. Despite our differences, though, I felt a kinship with my brothers and sisters deeper than anything I could put into words.

What were daily events for most other students were revelations for me. I was amazed, for example, at my first trip to a movie theater. Nor will I ever forget the movie I saw, *Live on the Sunset Strip*, or its star, Richard Pryor. I went alone on a Saturday during my first semester because I didn't want to embarrass myself. I didn't know the basics of moviegoing. Where do you pay? Where do you sit? And I couldn't admit to anyone that, at the age of eighteen, I'd never been in a theater before. I chose the Pryor movie because I had caught snatches of his act on television and was immediately drawn to his brilliant humor. I also chose Pryor, I suppose, because he had been strictly off limits in the Smiley household. He cursed freely, reason enough for Mama and Daddy to ban him.

The ticket booth seemed self-explanatory, but I remember being unsure, once inside, whether the ticket entitled me to popcorn or whether popcorn was extra. The dark cavernous theater itself was wondrous, with baroque décor and red velvet curtains reminiscent of cathedrals I had seen in photographs. Even watching the coming attractions was a novelty. The enormity of the screen was equally novel. But nothing had prepared me for the reality of seeing Pryor filmed in front of a live audience in Hollywood, California.

Because he spoke black, because he was a black man, like me, from a hick town—Pryor came from Peoria, Illinois—because everything he said spoke to the frustrations, fears, and oddities of being an outsider, a minority inside the majority culture, I connected with Pryor like crazy. The rhythm of his lightning-fast delivery, while a world away from Dr. King's, reflected a similar sense of pace and drama. The great African American standup comics preach, and Pryor preached with a power that quickly won me over. He was so smart. He was so funny. He did voices so well— old men in the barber shop, white squares, black pimps. He even gave voice to animals and body parts.

In 1982, I couldn't have told you that I found an artfulness in his vulgarity, but that's what I was sensing. His sexual storytelling had a literary quality I found fascinating. I also instinctively knew that Pryor represented *us*, all of African American culture. His ferocious energy was *our* energy. His perpetual horniness was *our* horniness. His worldview came from *our* dysfunctional homes, *our* mamas, *our* daddies, *our* churches, *our* dance halls, *our* bar rooms, *our* dreams, *our* drives, *our* need to be accepted and loved.

Pryor's humor cut deep. He moved me to tears, but tears, I now understand, that contained both sadness and joy. *Live on the Sunset Strip* was filmed after two seismic events in Pryor's life—accidentally setting himself on fire while cooking crack, and traveling to Africa. He saw both incidents through the lens of sly self-deprecation. In essence, he assaulted himself for being a fool. Pryor's near-death encounters reinforced my conviction that Mama's church was right about narcotics. Surely they separate us from God. The greater revelation for me, however, was Pryor's epiphany about the *n* word: "In Africa," he said, "I didn't see any niggers." In Africa, Pryor connected to the most profound part of his cultural heritage. Africa had him reexamining his sense of self. He discovered a beauty in blackness that went beyond clichés, slang, and street language. Watching Pryor, that beauty stirred my soul and awakened questions about my heritage that I was determined to get answers to.

Black music was another great awakening for me. Black gospel music, of course, had always been part of my life. But because Mama had kept secular music out of the trailer, I had missed the late 1960s movement that had produced the innovative work of Stevie Wonder and Marvin Gaye. In the 1970s, I knew only superficially the songs of singers like Teddy Pendergrass, the O'Jays, and other Philly International stars. I discovered Prince, with *Dirty Mind* and *Controversy*. *Purple Rain* was among the first films I saw at IU, and it rocked my world.

It was my black brothers and sisters at IU who showed me the spirit of black secular music as community. I was well aware of the black church community and its power to galvanize hearts. But the black community that bonded at a Maze concert, for example, opened my eyes to something entirely new and profound.

Maze and its great lead singer, Frankie Beverly, created a sort of secular church that I found myself joining. I'm proud to say I'm still a member of that church today. Its spirit feels as vital and sacred to me as the services at the New Bethel Tabernacle Church in Kokomo. Unlike George Clinton's Funkadelic or Maurice White's Earth, Wind & Fire, Beverly's Maze never found a big crossover audience. But that only added to its appeal. The band belonged to the black community. And its enduring anthems—"Workin' Together," "Golden Time of Day," "Joy and Pain," "Happy Feelings," "Back in Stride"—turned its concerts into giant family get-togethers. Maze's messages were always optimistic. *Hang in—things will get better.* Beverly's silky-smooth ballads and sophisticated funk transported me, providing a link between my Pentecostal past and my consciousness-raising present as a member of the black student community.

Nonetheless, there were divisions within the black community at IU. Many of the students had come to college through Upward Bound, a program for those whose high school education required supplemental help. I prided myself on not needing Upward Bound. My life experience might have paled next to that of the brothers and sisters from, say, Detroit, but my high school education was first-rate.

I attended a storefront congregation off campus whose church van came by to pick me up every Sunday. The pastor, Charles Finnell, had left a big church in Indianapolis to minister to students in Bloomington. The storefront had a Pentecostal bent but, unlike New Bethel Tabernacle in Kokomo, encouraged education. I felt at ease becoming part of a congregation that mirrored the kind I had grown up in—where God is celebrated with joy, music, and praise. I was also impressed that Finnell had gone from a big church in a big town to a small church in a small town in following what he felt was God's will. He loved students and never failed to ask during the service, "How many of you are from the university? Stand up and make yourself known. Know, too, that this is your spiritual home away from home. We're blessed to have you." Pastor Finnell did much to remind me that loving God and loving education were not mutually exclusive.

My appetite for extracurricular activity spilled over from high school to college. I joined the IU debate team my freshman year and began traveling to tournaments, arguing the intricate points of policies such as GATT, the General Agreement on Tariffs and Trade.

I was amazed to learn that there was an entire African American studies department at IU. Professor McElroy, my first black professor, taught Afro-American studies using a call-and-response style that made my heart sing. He didn't lecture; he provoked you into a dialogue. To be addressed as "Mr. Smiley" by an older and distinguished black teacher filled me with a sense of self-worth I had never before felt. Professor McElroy riffed on topics like a jazzman; later in life, I would find this same style emulated by Cornel West. When academics improvise in the mode of, say, Thelonious Monk, you can't stop listening and can't resist participating.

McElroy would jump from James Baldwin to James Joyce, from Miles Davis to Herman Melville, from Richard Wright and Ralph Ellison to Ralph Waldo Emerson. He took daring intellectual leaps, spanning the contributions of W. E. B. DuBois, the glories of the Harlem Renaissance, and the subtleties of Maya Angelou.

On the social front, I had no interest in joining a fraternity, despite their interest in me. The entire pledging process put me off. I didn't want the hazing. And yet, one fact gave me pause: Martin Luther King Jr. had been an Alpha at Morehouse. I realized that not all fraternities were suspect. Jesse Jackson, for example, was an Omega, as were many outstanding students and serious achievers.

Because of King, I was initially attracted to Alpha Phi Alpha, and the Alphas didn't hesitate to use King as a drawing card. But Kappa Alpha Psi seemed to have a stronger presence at IU. Competition among the fraternities was keen. The Kappas had a ready answer to King being an Alpha: "He was an Alpha at More-house," they were quick to point out, "not Indiana. If he'd come to Indiana, he'd be a Kappa." Kappa Alpha Psi, I learned, was founded at IU and was the only black fraternity with a house on fraternity row. Mayor Tom Bradley of Los Angeles, a man I greatly admired, was a Kappa.

While I still hadn't decided on a fraternity during my first se-mester, I had decided about one thing: I was not going home for Christmas. I still wasn't ready to go back for a family holiday. I missed everyone, but I had too many new ideas swirling around in my head that had little to do with the New Bethel Tabernacle Church, the center of the Smiley Christmas celebration. I didn't want to argue, I didn't want to react, I didn't want to be accused of being a deserter or a heathen. I just wanted to avoid the whole thing.

There was also the issue of my relationship with Mama and Dad. Since arriving in Bloomington, I had had no communication with them. They hadn't asked how I was doing or how I had man-aged to get into school without their help. They hadn't asked how I could afford to pay tuition. I would have thought they'd want to know. Looking back, I'm sure they did care, but pride and perhaps confusion kept them from getting involved. I suppose my own pride kept me from mentioning any of the good news to them. But in addition to my pride and family history, a romantic interest in a freshman coed from another school helped me decide to go to Michigan during Christmas.

Snow was falling hard. James Taylor's soothing voice played on the car radio as he sang "Sweet Baby James," describing the first December snow in the Berkshires of Massachusetts. I had never seen the Berkshires, but the road from Indiana up to Michigan was my own magical landscape. The snowfall was the first of the season. It was my first Christmas away from home. I was on my way to Muskegon, to stay with the family of my girlfriend, Jackie. I had originally met Jackie back in high school at a church convention. Beautiful and vivacious, she shared many of my values and dreams. We got along beautifully. Jackie was going to school at Michigan State, in East Lansing. My friend Rudy also had a girlfriend at Michigan State, and we were driving up together in his small car.

The Christmas holidays turned out to be everything I'd hoped for. Jackie's family had ten kids, just like my family. Jackie's mama cooked a fabulous dinner and went out of her way to make me feel welcome.

Back at school, my horizons continued to expand in any number of ways. I heard Joe Sample, the brilliant jazz pianist, play live at the IU auditorium. I was seduced by a sound the brothers from back East were talking about, Grandmaster Flash and the Furious Five. A new school was being born.

The old school was just as exciting. I heard Ray Charles in person for the first time when he came to our campus. The marriage of church and state in Ray's music was nothing less than a revelation to me—the way he secularized and sexualized gospel music and rhythm and blues. I had discovered new poets and writers that semester, such as seventeenth-century poet John Donne, who, like the Reverend Ray, combined physical and metaphysical imagery in celebration of the sacred and divine.

I heard black operatic star Leontyne Price in recital at the Indiana University concert hall, performing arias from *Aida*, *Tosca*, and *Madame Butterfly*. She was the first African American singer I knew who had mastered opera. I felt a mixture of surprise and pride hearing a black soprano embrace music and stories from a culture so far removed from the Mississippi home where she (and I) had been born. At the end of the concert, she sang "This Little Light of Mine," her mother's favorite spiritual. It brought me back home. I listened with tears in my eyes.

On the weekends, I sometimes went to a little club off campus called the Bluebird, a smoky hangout where the in-crowd came to drink beer and listen to rock music. I wasn't interested in the beer, but the rock 'n' roll was exciting. It was the first time I heard a young white rocker named John Cougar Mellencamp, who played a fiery mix of rhythm and blues and rock, overlaid with stories of the blue-collar, small-town landscape of the Midwest.

Traveling with the debate team to the major universities in Ohio, Michigan, and Nebraska, I argued esoteric policy issues, reading for the first time in my life magazines like *Time* and *Newsweek*, competing and sometimes besting guys from Harvard, Princeton, and Yale. For the first time in my life, I was able to attend big-time sporting events, especially Hoosier basketball, where Bobby Knight coached Indiana to national prominence.

My freshman year introduced me to an exciting, wider world I had had only glancing contact with before. That world took a darker turn my sophomore year. The tragic death that haunted Indiana's campus that year would change my perception of everything.

# RIP Denver Smith

Following my freshman year, I stayed in Bloomington during the summer, working and attending summer-school classes. I lived with Bobby Knight's basketball players off campus. It was an eye-opening experience. Just being around them conferred on me a kind of status by association, as well as introductions to a number of attractive women. Most of all, however, staying in Bloomington let me avoid a reunion with my family. I'd been introduced to so many new ideas and people that I wasn't ready to assimilate my new life as an IU student with my old.

At the beginning of the fall semester, I met a girl who lived in the dorm next to mine. As we began dating, and eventually became intimate, another of the prohibitions from my Pentecostal childhood fell away. Although romance and sex would continue to blossom in my life, they would never dominate it. Hard work, ambition, learning new things, and meeting new people consumed my interest. The Smiley & Sons work ethic never left me.

In the end, I pledged Kappa that fall semester, in part because the Kappas seemed the most involved in academic excellence and extracurricular accomplishment. But I hated the pledging process. The eight-week ritual was juvenile and had not enough to do with higher education. I hung in, however, and suffered the traditional humiliations, but I never became very active as an undergraduate. Later in life, membership in the fraternity came to mean more to me, especially in seeking help from a fellow Kappa in a strange city, and now I'm honored to help younger brothers trying to establish themselves. Today, I'm pleased to be a life member of my fraternity.

I never let fraternity life distract me into excessive partying. Some people succumbed. But college parties bored me. My own instincts led me, instead, into student government. I started out as the business manager of our dorm. Later, I was elected to the student senate, and eventually became director of minority affairs. While I was never active in the Black Student Union, as head of minority affairs for the predominantly white campus student government, I interacted with the BSU. But I was far more interested in making a mark in the larger university governing board. I had my sights set on Harvard Law School and working in Washington, D.C., after graduation. If you are going to set your sights, you might as well set them high.

My sights were suddenly altered, though, by an event none of us could have anticipated. I can still feel the shock of it today, twenty years later.

During my freshman year, I'd often wander off to the gym for a pickup game of basketball. One night I was feeling restless. I couldn't study—or didn't want to—and was looking for a distraction, a way to burn off energy. It was around 9 P.M. when I got to the gym. Apart from one other guy, the basketball court was empty. The other guy was a huge brother with a massive physique. He was sinking free throws effortlessly, one after another.

"You're Denver Smith, aren't you?" I asked him.

"That's me," he answered in a friendly tone.

"Tavis Smiley," I said.

"Good meeting you, Brother Tavis," he said, extending a soul handshake.

Denver Smith was a well-known athlete on campus. He was the starting middle guard on the IU football team. At nearly six feet and 250 pounds, he was physically intimidating. But his personal manner was just the opposite—he couldn't have been nicer.

"Interested in a little one on one?" he asked.

"Sure," I said.

I was skinny, not a half-bad player, but no match for Denver. For a big man, Denver was quick. He outmuscled me under the basket and outshot me both inside and out. The game wasn't even close, but we had a great workout. Denver was neither vicious nor cutthroat as a competitor. Fact is, he was a down-home brother who reminded me of my brother Garnie (who would soon come to IU and make the football team as a walk-on). Denver was all heart. Afterward, we sat by a vending machine and drank 7-UPs. I asked him where he grew up.

"Dayton," he said. "Played football at Meadowdale High School and won a scholarship to IU."

He was already married and, with his college football career now complete, was dreaming of playing in the NFL.

"So that's why you're working so hard to stay in shape," I said.

"Gotta defend my bench-press record in the weight room," he said with a big smile.

"What is your record?" I asked.

"Four hundred thirty pounds."

I shook my head in amazement.

"I've seen you around campus," he said to me. "Aren't you one of those debating brothers?"

"Trying."

"Where you from?"

"Kokomo area."

"Didn't think there were many black folk around there."

"There aren't."

Denver was interested in knowing what it was like being one of only a few black students in an otherwise all-white high school in Indiana.

After talking for ten minutes or so, Denver said, "All right, Tavis," when we had downed our soft drinks. "Let's do it again."

"Wish I could give you a little more competition."

"You're doing just fine," Denver assured me in his easygoing manner. "You got me working up a mean sweat."

Our subsequent game was a duplicate of the first. Denver beat my butt, but he did so good-naturedly. Afterward, we chewed the fat awhile longer. I felt like I'd made a friend.

The next summer, I'd often see Denver around school. He knew the basketball players I was living with, and occasionally we'd all hang out together. I never got especially close to him, but we knew and respected each other. Everyone who knew Denver couldn't help but like him.

At the start of the fall semester, I'd heard that Denver's wife, Cynequa, had given birth to a girl whom they named Ambrosia. Meanwhile, Denver worked out like crazy in the hopes of being recruited by the NFL.

On the evening of September 13, 1983, I was at the dorm with some friends. It was my birthday, although later I wouldn't remember that fact. We had ordered pizza and were watching the Monday Night Football game. When the game was over—the Chargers beat the Chiefs, as I recall—we were about to turn off the TV when the local news came on. Nothing's duller than the local news in Bloomington. But suddenly the anchorman mentioned Denver Smith's name.

"Indiana University football player Denver Smith was shot and killed at 3:15 this afternoon during a struggle with police behind the Service Control Center on South Henderson Street," he reported. "Two policeman fired two bullets each into Smith's back as he was on top of a third policeman, beating him with a nightstick. Police say Smith, twenty-four, was acting erratically and seemed to be deranged. Police had been called to the scene because a few minutes earlier Smith had stopped traffic by waving a tire iron at passing motorists."

I was stunned. The entire campus was stunned. How could this be? Denver Smith was the mellowest person I knew, a beautiful brother with a kicked-back attitude. He had never been known to take drugs. He was a good husband, a brand-new daddy, a man getting ready to move up to the NFL. He had his whole life in front of him.

"Denver Smith," the newscaster went on, "was shot in the back four times. The police are calling it self-defense."

Self-defense? Deranged behavior? Denver?

It didn't compute.


The death of Denver Smith galvanized the black student population of IU. The police claimed Denver was taking powerful drugs at the time of his death. But when the county coroner, a forensic pathologist, conducted an autopsy, a urine test indicated only that he had smoked marijuana within the past month. No alcohol, cocaine, or PCP was found in his system.

One reporter claimed Denver went into a rage after the side mirror of a city utilities truck grazed him lightly as the truck drove by. Again, that didn't sound like the Denver we knew and loved.

Something was wrong.

It was my first experience dealing with the kinds of real-life prejudices and policies that have incensed black people time and again. I couldn't help but be incensed myself. An unarmed black man was shot in the back by white cops. With only one exception, the Bloomington police force was all white. Everyone involved in the investigation was white. Moreover, the reported "facts" concerning Denver's death were marred by contradictions.

Until now, death had rarely been a part of my life. For me, college had been about new vistas and new possibilities. Denver's death reminded me of the earlier death of a friend whose passing I had all but blocked out.

It happened early in high school. Like me, Janet was one of the few black students in our class. I had a crush on her. If I had been allowed to date, I would have asked her out in a heartbeat. I'd fantasize that Janet was my steady girlfriend. Instead, we became close friends. Her dad, like mine, was stationed at the air-force base. We had a lot in common. She was a majorette who strutted in front of the marching band; I played second-chair saxophone. I couldn't keep my eyes off her. Then one day she didn't show up for our 8:30 algebra class. By noon that day, an announcement came over the PA system that the night before, Janet had been killed in a car crash. I was devastated. Several days later I went to the funeral, still in shock. When the services were over, I passed by the casket. I heard Joe Cocker singing "You Are So Beautiful" on an endless loop. To this day, I cannot bear to hear that song.

I couldn't fathom what it meant to die at such a young age. Somehow I had been able to push the memory of her death out of my mind. But with Denver's death, the sadness and sense of loss came rushing back. And this time another element was involved: race.

While Ralph, the grade school bully, had beaten me for weeks, he didn't do it because I was black. He beat me because he thought he could push me around. This was different. For the first time, I was seeing what I had been reading about in cities like Chicago and New York, how racial tension between white authority and the disenfranchised black population could explode into tragedy. I couldn't escape Denver's tragedy if I had wanted to. And I didn't want to. I wanted to get to the bottom of how he had died.

As a champion speaker, I was articulate and passionate in expressing my views. In the wake of Denver's death, I helped organize vigils and protest rallies. When questions needed to be asked, I asked them. When newspaper and television reporters came from Indianapolis looking for student reaction to the controversy, I was chosen as spokesperson. For the first time, I was quoted in the papers and interviewed on TV. I wasn't the least bit reticent.

The murder of Denver Smith turned me into an advocate for black rights. As the highest-ranking black person inside the student government infrastructure, I worked with Mark Russell, the president of the Black Student Union. Although Mark was an experienced inner-city kid and I was a hick from the sticks, Denver's death brought us together. We teamed up to take on the Bloomington establishment and found ourselves confronting city officials all the way up to the mayor.

In the end, the three policemen involved in Denver's shooting were exonerated. Denver's widow, Cynequa, filed a suit of negligence in a U.S. district court in Indianapolis. A six-member jury found for the policemen and the city of Bloomington. Her appeal of the ruling failed.

But the black student population of IU was never the same again. Even though we didn't get the result we sought, we saw we had the power to attract media attention and force officials to the table. New recommendations were made—and many enforced—concerning police hiring practices. More minorities were employed. Training methods were scrutinized and modernized. The cautionary words of the only black officer on the force, Charlie Brown, were heeded. Brown claimed it wasn't racism that motivated his fellow officers' actions, but poor preparation. Brown argued that Denver should have been spoken to from a distance, not assaulted.

We were surprised and heartened to see IU president John Ryan attend a memorial service for Denver at the Black Culture Center. That day, Ryan promised a university scholarship for Denver's daughter, Ambrosia. (Eighteen years later, that promise was kept, though only at the insistence of William Wiggins, a black professor and one of my favorite teachers at IU. The Afro-American Affairs Department located Ambrosia, and she attended IU on scholarship. Much later in my life, after I gave a speech in Chicago, a woman and daughter approached me. "I'm Cynequa Smith," the older woman said, "and this is Ambrosia." The three of us embraced and cried.)

For his big-hearted warmth and extraordinary athletic talent, Denver Smith will always be remembered. I'll never know—we'll never know—what truly happened that day back in September of 1983. But one thing is sure. Lives were changed by Denver's tragic death, my own included. His legacy lives on, and the advocacy he helped to spark is now a permanent part of our community's commitment to justice.

## Madam Mayor

Sophomore year I went home for the holidays. I hadn't seen my family in over a year. When I arrived in the early afternoon, the house was almost empty. My siblings were at school, Dad was at work, and Mama was out shopping.

"I can tell it's you, Tavis," Big Mama called from the back bedroom. "I'd know those footsteps anywhere."

"And I'd know your voice anywhere," I said, entering the room.

My grandmother was seated in an easy chair next to her bed. She was reading the Bible. A spirited Albertina Walker gospel tape was playing on the machine behind her.

We hugged and kissed, and I held her for a long, long time.

Big Mama had never been far from my mind. Lord, how I loved her. And I knew that she was the key to constructing a reconciliation between my mother and me.

"It's so good to have my baby back," she said. "Hear you been making a name for yourself at that fancy college."

"Where'd you hear that?"

"Your mama and daddy talk about you all the time."

"They do?"

"Sure they do. They're mighty proud."

"I don't believe it."

"Boy, you gotta believe Big Mama 'cause Big Mama's got no reason to lie."

"They've never said anything to me."

"Sometimes it's easier for folk to brag on their children to other folk. Sometimes it's not easy to tell your own children what you think of them."

"I don't understand," I said.

"Well, just like that, children move out, go off to college, get a life of their own. Not easy for mamas and daddies to let go. You're doing something they never did. You're going places they never been."

"But, Big Mama, you didn't act like them and get all disapproving when I went off. You understood. You gave me your blessing and even slipped me a little money."

Big Mama laughed that infectious laugh of hers before saying, "Easiest job in the world is being a grandmother. I don't gotta raise you. I just gotta love you."

"You do the best job of that of any grandmother I know."

"And so do your daddy and mama. Don't ever think they don't love you, boy, 'cause they love you just as hard as they can."

"I don't know . . ."

"Let's pray," said Big Mama. She took my hand and began, "Father God, we praise you, we exalt you, we thank you for every little thing and every big thing in our life. We thank you, Father, for our health, the food we eat, the air we breathe, the rising sun in the morning, and the moonlight at night. We thank you for your mercy, and we thank you for your grace. We thank you for each other, Father, and the strength we share—brother to brother, sister to sister, father to mother, mother to son. I thank you, Father, that you have blessed me with my family and my beautiful grandchildren. May they all prosper, and may they each, in their own way, glorify you. But mostly, Father, I thank you for Jesus and his sacrifice, for sending down the Holy Ghost—praise God!—and setting us all free. Yes, Lord, we are free, Father God, to do your will. Amen."

"Amen," I echoed.

Later that day my brothers came home, and we all high-fived and hugged each other madly. When Mama and Dad arrived, there was an awkward moment between us. Then Dad shook my hand and put his arm around my shoulder. Mama kissed me. We looked at each other and I tried to smile. But I still felt the tension.

During the Denver Smith protests, I served on a university committee that met with the mayor of Bloomington, Tomilea Allison, a white woman. When I argued our position and expressed my doubts about the official findings, the mayor was responsive. She saw me as a serious citizen, a student of political science and public policy. Afterward, much to my amazement, she offered me a work-study internship in her office. I quickly accepted. Working in a councilman's office in Kokomo had opened my eyes to the daily workings of government. This was like an entire university education.

I wrote letters to constituents, did research for the mayor, and helped develop position papers on local issues. It was exciting stuff. But I broke the law in the course of performing my job in a manner that still haunts me to this day.

I padded my time sheets. I was getting paid five dollars an hour. I figured that putting down three hours of work when I only worked two wasn't going to break the city bank. And before long, I made a regular habit of adding a half hour here and an hour there.

One day the deputy mayor sternly said, "Mr. Smiley, come into my office."

By then I'd been working in the mayor's office for several months. Unlike the mayor, the deputy mayor was not a fan of mine. A big-bellied man with a strong distaste for bright students with big ambitions, he had been keeping his own time card on me. He noticed how I had slightly but consistently inflated my hours. The man had charted out my time and calculated the cost of my padded hours down to the last dime.

"This is serious business, Mr. Smiley," he said. "Have you ever broken the law before?"

My mind raced back to the time I'd taken a pair of sunglasses from a store. But my parents had made me return the glasses, and the store owner had accepted my apology.

"No, I haven't," I said.

"We have several choices here, Mr. Smiley. We could report this to the university and ask for your immediate expulsion. Or we could turn the matter over to the district attorney and press charges."

I suddenly saw my brief life flash before me. I could see the headlines in newspapers from Kokomo to Bloomington: "Star Student Indicted! Tavis Smiley a Fraud!" I suddenly saw my parents crying out, "Not again! First he humiliates us in front of our entire church! Now he humiliates us in front of the entire state!"

"What do you have to say for yourself, Mr. Smiley?" the deputy mayor said, glaring at me with angry eyes.

"I don't . . . I don't know what to say."

"I've submitted my findings to the mayor. She wants to see you, alone, in her office, tomorrow, 9 A.M. sharp."

That night I couldn't sleep. I imagined the worst; my future was in tatters before me. How could I have done this? At the time, the fudging I'd done on my hours hardly seemed like cheating. If I had added twenty hours over the intervening months, as the deputy had figured, the money came to one hundred dollars. Was I going to prison over a hundred dollars? And yet I knew what I'd done was wrong—I'd broken the law. The deputy mayor had reminded me that drug dealers had been slain over smaller amounts. I wasn't sure of the analogy, but was in no position to argue.

Next morning I wore my lone suit to work. I hoped that my suit and tie would show how eager I was to make amends.

I knocked on the mayor's door.

"Come in, Tavis."

The mayor sat at a small conference table and motioned for me to sit across from her.

"If this report is true, I'm disappointed in you, Tavis. Is it true?"

"Yes, it is," I admitted, my eyes lowered in shame.

"Well, then." The mayor took a deep breath. "I placed great trust in you, Tavis. I saw you as a bright young man. I never suspected you'd take advantage of this office."

"I'm so sorry, Mayor Allison . . ."

"More than taking advantage of this office," she continued, "you betrayed the trust of the people of this city. In essence, you stole their money. Is that clear?"

"Yes, Your Honor."

"The point is this: In public service, you can never betray the public's trust, even over a single dime."

"I understand that now."

"To correct this wrong, Tavis, I'm ordering you to work off those twenty hours you added illegally. Once you've completed that work, the people's money will effectively be repaid. The matter will end there. Furthermore, I see no reason for any of this to leave this office. I've instructed the deputy mayor to close the case on the promise that you will make up your hours."

"I promise to do so, Your Honor."

"Good. And I trust, Tavis, that of all the things you've learned working in this office, this unfortunate incident will be the most useful. If it keeps you on the straight and narrow, it'll be a lesson for the rest of your life."

As Big Mama loved to say, there's a lesson and a blessing in every misfortune. I vowed to never stray or betray the public's trust again.

# End of the Road

I don't believe it," I told my father. He had called me at my dorm one day during my junior year. I knew something was wrong because Dad rarely made long-distance calls.

"I'm afraid it's true, Tabo."

"Just like that?"

"Just like that. We've reached the end of our road together."

My father was calling to say he and my mother were separating.

My reaction was absolute shock. If there was one certain fact in this uncertain world, it was this: Mama and Daddy would be married for the rest of their days. Never once had I seen indications otherwise. They didn't argue or fight. They didn't disappear on each other. They gave no hint of anything but marital unity.

I felt like I'd been hit over the head with a ton of bricks. "Why? What happened?"

"Nothing I could explain over the phone. We're just going our separate ways, that's all."

The truth is that my parents never really offered me an explanation. One after another, my siblings called me at school for a reality check. Like me, they were incredulous. They'd had no warnings, seen no clues. Where had been the discord that had led not merely to disagreement but to my father moving out?

All Dad said was, "Too much of anything can get old." But when I asked him directly if he was talking about my mother or their church or his unyielding sense of familial duty, I never got an answer. All he said was that he was moving to a small place around the corner from Mama and that nothing would be all that different.

But, of course, everything *was* different. My view of my folks had shifted entirely. Their separation had shaken one of the pillars of my emotional life. I thought they were devoted to each other. Only as I lived with the idea awhile and discussed it with my brothers and sisters did I start to see their relationship more clearly. My mother was a hard-driving woman. Her whole life was—and is—God. That's wonderful, but it left only a limited amount of time for Dad. Only a certain kind of man can fit into that emotional world. My father surely tried. He accepted everything my mother brought to the marriage, beginning with me, a child she had conceived with another man. He accepted her four nieces and nephews into our lives. He accepted her mother. He accepted her insistence on strictness to keep us kids on the right path. He went along with her entire program and worked his behind off to provide for our crew. But eventually he tired of the program. I know I had. I felt for his fatigue.

I never asked whether he had had any indiscretions. It wasn't something I felt a son could ask his father. And besides, for all my feelings of sympathy, the scars and sting of the beating that put me in the hospital still loomed large in my memory.

But I felt, too, for my mother. I knew the toll it must be taking on her. And I knew she'd never marry again. In some way, she was married to Jesus. Mama's standards were so high no mere mortal could meet them.

Our family dynamic was shifting in a profound and permanent way. Little by little, as my father moved out as head of the household and I learned to deal with finances, I took on a leadership role. It began at college. By my junior year, I had generous scholarships from being on the debate team. From time to time, I was able to actually give Mama a little money. In various ways I helped my siblings make their college plans. Later, when I was out in the world working, I paid their tuition. Subtly, imperceptibly, I began to replace my father as the head of the household.

In my junior year, my extracurricular activities distracted me from my studying. For a time, I was put on scholastic probation. I had to buckle down with the books. I worked like a dog until I had raised my grades and was back in the good graces of the university.

At the start of second semester that year, however, I made a trip to the West Coast that changed everything. It was a trip that turned me around and sent me in a completely different direction.

# Urban Angels

W hen you're cruising down Pacific Coast Highway, riding shotgun in a convertible on a 75-degree January afternoon with the sun shining down and a gentle ocean breeze caressing your face, it's hard not to love Los Angeles.

The palm trees, the mountains, the relaxed attitude, Maze's "Golden Time of Day" playing on the radio—I was one happy brother when I hit the City of Angels for the first time.

I had come to L.A. to attend a national convention of student leaders. My college roommate and close friend Chi, who was also on the trip, had a cousin named Tamara, who lived in L.A. She picked us up at the airport and showed us the town. I thought I had died and gone to heaven. When I left Bloomington, it was 15 degrees, the streets a sheet of ice. Here there was nothing but blue ocean and beaches crowded with girls in halter tops.

Several student leaders I met from various sections of the country were taking off a semester from their senior year and finding accredited internships in Washington, D.C. The federal government was encouraging them, and we all thought such positions might lead to prestigious posts after graduation.

"Don't believe it," said one brother from Michigan who had done it. "I spent a semester pushing paper in the State Department. It got me nowhere. Even worse, it's more boring than working at the post office. Washington is one big bureaucracy. Internships in Washington are a one-way ticket to Dullsville."

The brother's words made an impression. The more I talked to students who had actually interned in D.C., the more I was convinced that his experience was the norm. No one seemed to benefit from interning for the government.

All this was on my mind when Tamara asked me if I wanted to meet Jim Brown, the legendary former Cleveland Browns running back and movie star. Of course. Who wouldn't want to meet Jim Brown?

So Tamara, Chi, and I headed over there, her little VW Rabbit climbing higher and higher through the Hollywood hills. We pulled up to the driveway, got out of the car, and knocked on the front door. "It's open," a loud voice boomed.

Brown and some friends were playing backgammon in the den. "Before you meet Jim," said Tamara, "take a look at the view from the patio."

The view was breathtaking. I could hardly contain my excitement. The enormous city spread before me like a dream. My own dreams—of being successful, of righting society's wrongs, of advocating on behalf of others—boiled up inside me. I could see all the way to the ocean. Like the vista, life itself seemed unlimited in its possibilities. As day began to fade to dusk and the sky turned a burnished gold, a bold idea hit me, an idea about Los Angeles and its mayor, Tom Bradley.

In 1985, Tom Bradley was among the top black politicians in the country. The year before, he and Peter Ueberroth had put on the Summer Olympics and wound up bringing the city a $200 million surplus. The feat was unprecedented, and in part because of its success, Bradley was touted as one of the shrewdest and most effective leaders anywhere. What better way to enter big-time politics than to work for Tom Bradley? It would be a million times better than interning in D.C., where I was sure to get lost in the bureaucratic maze.

Somehow, someway, I had to convince Bradley to hire me.

But where to begin? How to set the gears in motion? My only advantage was that Bradley was a Kappa. In fact, he'd been national president of the fraternity. How could I penetrate his inner circle and let him know that I existed, much less qualify for an internship in his administration?

"Come meet Jim," said Tamara, snapping my daydream.

Inside the house, Tamara introduced me to Jim Brown as a "national student leader." I was a little embarrassed but also pleased when Brown said, "That's great. We need more young men like you. Meet my friend George Hughley."

Hughley had played for the Washington Redskins. Like Brown, he was a real brother.

"So what's a national student leader from Indiana doing here in L.A.?" he asked me.

"Trying to find a way to meet Mayor Bradley."

Hughley smiled, let a second or two go by, and then said, "I work for Tom Bradley."

In the face of good news, Big Mama used to say, "This is the kind of God we serve."

*This is the kind of God we serve*, I thought the next day, as George Hughley picked me up and drove me over to city hall to personally introduce me to the people in charge of internships.

It was all too much, but that's the kind of God we serve. One minute I was asking myself how I could hook up with the Bradley administration, the next minute I was inside the mayor's offices. In the distance it took to walk from the patio to the den of Jim Brown's house, my life had been reordered.

Hughley introduced me to a battery of officials. The man in charge of interns, Craig Lawson, told me, "Son, write me a letter when you get back to school, and we'll give you every consideration."

In my wild optimism and excitement, I didn't hear his words, "We'll give you every consideration." What I heard was, "This is a done deal." I saw myself inside city hall, impressing the powers that be, a young man on the rise, a brother who couldn't be denied.

Back in Bloomington, I began a take-no-prisoners assault on Mayor Bradley's office. I initiated a letter-writing blitz, closing with what I hoped was a masterpiece of etiquette and reason:

> *Mr. Mayor, whatever talents I may possess for organization, working with people, and executing ideas are at your disposal. What follows is a three-page detailed list of my qualifications, experience, and academic honors.*
>
> *I hope to hear from you soon, and thank you in advance for your confidence in me.*

I sent a letter to the mayor, as well as to Craig Lawson and everyone else I had met in city hall.

But this was just my opening. Every week, without fail, I wrote another letter to the mayor. Every week, without fail, I sent a reminder to his staff. I appealed to Mayor Bradley and his officials not only through letters but with faxes and phone calls and even telegrams. I bombarded Bradley's office as they had never been bombarded before. I had decided my future lay in the Los Angeles city hall, and I was determined to meet my future.

As my junior year proceeded, I continued my assault. If anything, I picked up the pace. When I received no response from the mayor or his deputies, I decided to spend my own money and fly out to Los Angeles to restate my position in person.

When I arrived, I couldn't get any of the officials on the phone. So I went over to city hall and headed directly to the mayor's suite of offices. A friendly black officer, Herman Walton, guarded the main door.

"Oh, so you're the famous Tavis Smiley," he said with a smile when I announced myself. "You're the boy sending those letters."

"Yes, sir."

"Well, son, I'm sorry but I've been told not to let you in."

"Why?" I asked.

"The people inside say go back to Indiana, and they'll let you know as soon as they get around to giving out those jobs."

"I can't see them? I can't talk to them personally?"

"Sorry, brother, I'd love to let you in, but it would cost me *my* job."

And so it was back to square one. After another month in Bloomington, another month with no news, I decided to fly back to L.A. on the red-eye. This time they'd see how passionate and determined I was. They'd have to let me in.

And there I was again, facing Officer Walton.

"Lord, have mercy," he said. "My favorite college student is back. You have a letter admitting you?"

"I have every confidence that someone in the mayor's office would be willing to see me."

"I know you're confident, Tavis," said Walton, "and confidence is a great thing. But I need some kind of permit to let you through these doors."

"What if I just waited out here, Officer Walton, until the mayor or one of his assistants came out?"

"I believe they call that loitering, son."

"What if you sent a message in to them?"

"I could do that."

"Just tell them Tavis Smiley is here."

"I do believe they are familiar with your name."

Walton went in. When he returned a few seconds later, he was shaking his head. "Sorry, son," he said. "Everyone's busy today."

"What about tomorrow?"

"It's a busy week."

"Thank you for your trouble, Officer Walton."

"Wish I could help."

"You tried."

"Don't give up," he urged.

"I won't," I assured him.

"That's the spirit."

The flight back was bumpy and long.

Winter melted into spring, and spring was about to burn into summer. Come September, I was determined to be living in Los Angeles, spending the first semester of my senior year interning for Mayor Bradley. But here it was May, and there was no word from the West Coast.

Four of my brothers came to live with me in Bloomington that summer. I loved reuniting with my siblings. I had a chance to act

as big brother. We were the boxcar children again—out of the boxcar of the trailer and now living in my small apartment, free of our
parents, on our own.

My brothers knew of my dream to work in L.A.—it's all I
talked about—and, like me, they were absolutely certain it was going to happen. It was just a question of getting that phone call.

The phone call never came. But a letter did, bearing an official
seal and a return address that read "City of Los Angeles."

It was one of those clear early days of summer when the world
seemed calm and the future filled with promise. I was walking
down the street toward our apartment when I heard my brothers
screaming at me from the open window, "It's here, Tavis! The letter's here! Hurry! Open it! Your letter from city hall is here!"

I rushed upstairs into my apartment, grabbed the letter, and
tore it open. I felt the thick government paper, saw the city seal,
saw that the letter contained three paragraphs. That was a good
sign at least. I wasn't being brushed off. They must have written a
thoughtful letter telling me when and where I could start. With my
heart hammering inside my chest, I read the words as quickly as I
could, but not so quickly as to misunderstand the meaning.

Dear Mr. Smiley,

The mayor and his staff have received your many letters
over these months and appreciate the time you have taken
to show your interest in our city government.

We have not replied until now, not because we do not
recognize your eagerness, but simply because we have been
overwhelmed by work. I hope you understand.

As much as we would like to accommodate you, unfortunately at this time all our intern appointments have been

*filled. Thank you, though, for your application, and we wish you the best in your collegiate career.*

*Sincerely,*
*Craig Lawson*

My brothers began pelting me with questions.

"What'd he say?" they asked.

"You get the job, Tav?"

"When are you leaving for L.A.?"

I dropped the letter on the floor numbly, my eyes filled with tears. My brothers scrambled to pick it up and read it. Then silence captured the room. No one said a word.

# Hustle and Flow Revisited

Ideally, you hustle and the results start flowing. You hustle and the world starts moving your way. You hustle, you work hard, you stay focused, and you get what you need. You gain from your pain. That's the ideal.

But the reality for a twenty-one-year-old kid from Bunker Hill, Indiana, looking to break into big-time politics in a city far from home at a ridiculously early age is that the hustle never stops. You can't trust any force other than your own determination. You have to be beside yourself with hustle, convinced that if you try hard enough, you can get where you want to go.

When I got the rejection letter, right in front of my brothers, I broke down and cried. They tried to console me, telling me it'd be all right, I'd get over it, something good would come of all of this. I knew they meant well, but I just couldn't hear it at that moment. I just needed to be left alone. "Y'all go out in the yard," I said. "I just need to think."

In truth, I didn't really need to think. Thinking only made it worse. Thinking made me feel my life was over. Thinking only heightened the despair. I had built up Los Angeles as the key to my future. No one could have campaigned as diligently as I had. No one could have had my qualifications. I was willing to work night and day.

*All our intern appointments have been filled.* There was no room to maneuver there. No "maybe later." No "if there's a cancellation, we will contact you." Just plain good-bye and good luck.

I felt a desperate need to get out of that apartment, get out of Bloomington, go somewhere, anywhere, away from the awful certainty of that letter. So I sent my brothers back to Kokomo, got into my old Datsun 280Z, and drove off. I had no idea where I was going. I didn't care. The afternoon was hot and humid. By the time I hit the highway, a thunderstorm had broken. Rain was slashing down. Out on I-70, driving too fast, paying no attention to the treacherous weather, I looked to my right and saw a huge eighteen-wheeler by my side. Tears streaming down my cheeks, I knew what I wanted to do: turn the wheel and drive my car into the trailer and end the whole thing, right there. I tried to turn the steering wheel—or thought I did. But the wheel wouldn't turn. It was stuck. Or perhaps God put his hand on the wheel as if to say, "No, not now, Tavis." Angry, I tried again, but the wheel wouldn't budge. I tried a third time. But the wheel would only steer straight ahead. The trailer pulled ahead of me, and the moment passed.

I was crying like a baby, gnashing my teeth, screaming to the dark skies. I was driving to nowhere, driving until the tank was nearly empty, and then filling it up and driving some more. I had driven most of the night when I realized I was starving. I stopped at a White Castle and downed a dozen little burgers. Afterward I went to a pay phone and made a collect call to a friend in St. Louis,

Danny Davis. I'd met Danny at a church convention. He was ten years older than me, married, someone I saw leading a stable life.

His wife Carol answered the phone. She heard I wasn't right.

"What happened, Tavis?" she asked.

"Nothing I can talk about right now, Carol. Is Danny around?"

"He'll be back in a little while."

"Well, I'm not far from St. Louis, Carol. I need to see him."

"Then come over, Tavis," she urged. "I'll give you directions."

When I arrived, I practically fell into Danny's arms. He gave me the biggest hug of my life. "What happened, brother?" he asked. "You look like you've been to hell and back."

I told him the story, in crushing detail.

"I know it's not easy," said Danny, "but you just got to chill, Tavis. You got to get your good senses back. Stay here for a while, brother, and just relax. Like the Bible says, joy comes in the morning."

When I opened my eyes in the morning, I was hungover with grief. My despair still lingered. But after Danny cooked us a beautiful big breakfast, I found myself feeling a little calmer. That's when an idea popped into my head. Rather than continue to mourn the loss of this opportunity, I'd give it another go. I'd write another letter.

This letter, though, wouldn't be formal, like the others. It wouldn't even be typed. I would write it in longhand, from the heart.

*Dear Mayor Bradley,*

*I don't know how many letters I've written you. Maybe thirty. Maybe forty. I don't even know if they've given you my letters. I don't even know if they've told you that I've flown from Indiana to L.A. twice at my own expense, just to make my case. I want to work for you more than anything in the world. Craig Lawson has written that he's already hired all the interns for the year, but I want to take this final opportunity to tell you, Mr. Mayor, that no one— no one on Planet Earth—will work for you with the dedication and passion and enthusiasm I'm offering. If this letter looks smudged, those smudges are from the tears rolling down my face. Those are tears, Mr. Mayor, of desire, tears born of a determination, tears of faith. I pray that somehow, someway, this letter from my heart will reach yours.*

*Sincerely,*
*Tavis Smiley*

I showed the letter to Danny. He said, "Don't change a word. Just mail it."

But before I left the house to drop it in a mailbox, Danny stopped me. "Let's pray first, Tavis."

"You pray for me, Danny."

"Father," he began, "I just want to thank you for Tavis and his friendship and all the friendships and fellowship that you create. You work through us, Father, and you make us better. You inspire us, and you make us inspire others. Whatever happens with Tavis, Father, he has inspired me. You've put your Spirit in him, and I know he's going to spread that Spirit all over the world, whether in California or Kalamazoo. Amen."

"Amen," I whispered.

I stayed in St. Louis for the weekend. When I got back to

Bloomington, I was feeling better. I was reconciled to the fact that God, not me alone, was in charge of my future. I was finally able to surrender.

My brothers returned for the rest of the summer. I went back to the books and concentrated on my studies as never before.

A month passed, and I realized that Los Angeles wasn't happening. I also realized I could live with that hard reality.

Then one afternoon, as I was walking back to our apartment, my brothers leaned out the window as they saw me approaching.

"Run!" they screamed hysterically.

"Get in here, Tavis!"

"Why?" I asked.

"Mayor Bradley is on the phone!"

I ran inside, breathless. "Hi, it's Tavis," I said.

"This is Tom Bradley."

"Yes, Mr. Bradley, I mean, Mr. Mayor."

"How are you, young man?"

"Fine, sir."

"I got your letter."

"I'm glad."

"I can't believe you've gone to so much trouble just to get an internship in my office."

"Well, sir, it means a lot to me."

"I can see that. You understand, of course, that these internships are not paid."

"I do understand, sir."

"How will you manage to live here, Tavis?"

"I'll find a way, sir, I guarantee you I will. When I arrived at IU, Mr. Mayor, I showed up with only a letter of acceptance. I had no scholarship, no money, no dorm assignment. But I've made my way. And I'm sure I'll make my way in Los Angeles."

"I have no doubt," the mayor chuckled. "And I understand that you're a good Kappa brother."

"I am, Mr. Mayor."

"Well, Tavis Smiley," he said, "anybody who went through what you went through to get an unpaid internship deserves one. I'm having my man Bill Elkins call you. He'll work out the details."

"I can't thank you enough, Mr. Mayor."

"I look forward to meeting you in person, Tavis."

"It will be my honor."

I put down the phone and screamed perhaps the loudest scream ever heard in the state of Indiana. In our boxcar apartment, my brothers and I jumped up and down like giddy schoolboys. Later, I called Big Mama to tell her the news.

"That's the kind of God we serve," she said.

That night I couldn't sleep. My dreams were coming true. I got up and began packing.

California, here I come.

# Urban Angels Revisited

I spent the next two mornings in Bloomington with my bags packed, staring at the phone, waiting for Bradley's assistant, Bill Elkins, to call. On Friday, he did.

"Mr. Smiley, this is Bill Elkins. The mayor tells me that you and I need to talk. I understand you're a Kappa."

"I am," I confirmed.

"That makes three of us—you, the mayor, and myself."

"I love it," I said.

"Now the mayor said that you'd like an internship sometime in the future."

"Yes, but actually not sometime in the future. I was thinking more like right away."

"The summer's nearly over, Mr. Smiley. I'm thinking we could get you an internship a year from now. We'll put you in our file and write you, say, in eight or nine months. Or if you're going to be in L.A. any time in the future, I'm happy to sit down and talk with you."

"I do plan to be in L.A., Mr. Elkins."

"When?"

"Monday."

"Monday?"

"Yes, sir, I'll be at your office Monday morning. Just tell me what time."

"Isn't Monday too soon?"

"I already have my ticket, Mr. Elkins."

"Well, if that's the case, I'll see you Monday at ten."

I scrambled to buy a ticket. The cheapest was a red-eye that landed at LAX at eight o'clock Monday morning. George Hughley said he'd pick me up and run me right over there. The plane was late and we barely got to city hall in time. When I arrived in front of the mayor's suite, Officer Walton was waiting. This time he was all smiles.

"I got the word, Tavis," he said, "and I personally want to be the one who opens the door for you."

He opened the door with a flair and said, "Go right in. The mayor's staff is waiting."

I met with Elkins first. After we greeted each other, I told him, "Mr. Elkins, I can't wait till next summer. I can't wait another year. I need to work for the mayor now."

"You might miss a semester of school," he said. "There's not enough time to guarantee that the internship will count as college credit."

"That's okay," I said. "I'll make up the credits. I don't want to be overly assertive, Mr. Elkins, but it has to happen now."

"Well, let's see what we can work out. Wait here, please."

Elkins got up and opened a connecting door to another office.

I heard him say, "Tom, that kid from Indiana is here. The one you called."

"I just called him the other day. Why is he here this soon?"

"I don't know," said Elkins. "But I think you should come in here and meet him."

Seconds later, the mayor appeared at the door. An immaculately dressed man with ramrod posture, at six feet six inches, Tom Bradley towered over us. His bearing was absolutely Lincolnesque.

"I'm happy to meet you, Tavis," he said.

"It's an honor to meet you, sir."

"So I hear you'd rather begin working sooner than later."

"Yes, sir. I'm flying back to Bloomington to pick up my car and driving back out. I'll be ready to work a week from today."

"You are one motivated young man, and I'm pleased you've aimed your sights in our direction. Before you leave, though, I want you to meet my staff. Your campaign to win this internship has made you something of a legend around here. But until now, son, no one has known what you look like. Bill, call in the staff."

The staff was ushered in. Because I had written each of them so many times, I knew all of their names already. But the one person I was looking for the hardest didn't come in until the very end.

"Mr. Smiley," Elkins said to me, "I want you to meet Craig Lawson. Craig, you'll be pleased to learn that Mr. Smiley is our newest intern. He was personally chosen by Mayor Bradley."

Craig Lawson looked like he wanted to pee down his leg.

"Good to meet you, sir," I said warmly, flashing him the biggest smile of my young life.

---

My last days in Bloomington were frantic. Armed with a letter from Mayor Bradley confirming my internship, I was able to get the university to preapprove the job as college credit. But how in the world would I support myself in L.A. while holding on to this unpaid position? No scholarship would cover the cost. Fortunately my hustle energy kicked into fifth gear. I sent a copy of Mayor Bradley's letter to each member of the Bloomington Community Progress Council, an organization that I had staffed made up of community leaders looking for worthwhile causes. I knew these people well. I hoped that my cause might prove worthy to them. And it did. I was pleased and relieved when they gave me five thousand dollars for living expenses. I took the money and bought new tires for my Datsun, packed my things into the car, and headed west. Where would I live when I got there? With no income and the price of L.A. housing sky high, how could I manage? I had no idea.

Nonetheless I arrived in the Big Orange happy as a lark. I remember speeding into the L.A. city limits on Interstate 10 listening to John Mellencamp's "Pink Houses" on the radio, telling the story of a black man with a black cat living in a black neighborhood with an interstate running through his front yard. "Ain't that America," he sang, "home of the free? Little pink houses for you and me."

I loved the idea of my man Mellencamp serenading me from mid-America as I entered the palm-tree-lined boulevards of L.A.

I got off the highway to fill up with gas and found myself in the shadow of downtown L.A. At the corner of Figueroa and Adams, I looked up at the great skyscrapers in the distance. I had made it to the big city, where I'd soon be working for the mayor. The road to my future was opening before me like the yellow brick road. When I tried pumping gas, nothing came out. Tried again, but again nothing.

"This is L.A., buddy," an attendant yelled at me, noticing my Indiana license plate. "We don't trust nobody. You gotta pay first."

Absentmindedly, I took out ten dollars, laid my wallet on the roof of the car, and went inside to pay. Inside, I heard the same attendant yelling at me again. "Buddy, someone's running off with your wallet!"

In a panic, I turned to see a short guy racing across the street. I realized that inside my wallet was all my cash—nearly five thousand dollars.

I raced after him. Frantically, he jumped on a bus before I could get to him.

"Stop!" I screamed at the bus driver as I ran alongside the bus. "Let me on! That man's got my money!"

But the bus driver couldn't hear me, and the bus was soon roaring down the road. I raced back to my car and put it in gear, burning rubber to chase down the bus. I refused to let the bus out of my sight. I honked my horn like a madman, looking desperately for a cop, but there were no cops around. I thought of ramming into the bus to get the bus to stop, but I couldn't get close enough; there was too much traffic. I was weaving in and out of traffic, frantic to keep up with the bus, to make the bus driver aware of me. I was hoping the thief would get off the bus so I could nail him, but he didn't; the bus kept on rolling.

Just as I was about to catch the bus, I was caught by a red light. I rolled down my window, screaming to whoever would listen: "Stop that bus! That man has my money!" I raced through red lights, I made crazy maneuvers—anything to catch the bus. I just couldn't lose that money—that money was my life. Up ahead, the bus was going faster, and I was losing it.

Then, way off in the distance, I saw it stop and saw someone getting off. It was him! The thief was getting off!

I spotted him running across a yard. So I ditched my car and took off after him. Fortunately, I was young and in shape and he was older and getting winded. We climbed over fences, jumped over hedges, and dashed through yards. I could see I was gaining on him. Finally, he threw down my wallet and ran on. I picked it up and—miracle of miracles!—all the money was there. So I let him go and hurried back to my car, half expecting my car to be stolen, but it was still there. Panting, on the verge of collapse, I heard a little voice inside my head say, "Welcome to L.A."

Given his tough-guy reputation, you wouldn't look at Jim Brown and think of an angel. But that is what he was for me when I moved to California. In September 1985, he let me live as his guest for the entire month, free of charge. Moreover, he turned what could have been a time of loneliness and uncertainty into a visit of welcome and warmth, not to mention excitement. Every night when I returned home from the mayor's office, Jim would be entertaining friends, everyone from Magic Johnson to Kareem Abdul-Jabbar. Brother Minister Louis Farrakhan was a visitor from time to time.

After leaving Jim's place, I connected with the Kappas at USC and ultimately lived in their fraternity house, where the rent was reasonable. In large measure, my personal life was in order. My professional life, however, was anything but.

The problem was that the mayor was on the third floor, but Elkins had put me on the twenty-second floor in the Office of Youth Development. That sounded interesting, but the work was not fulfilling. I never saw Bill Elkins or the mayor. I was far from the center of power and miserable as a result. But how could I complain? I was an intern, and interns can't be choosy. An intern has no right to go to his boss and lament his lack of access to the movers and shakers. But I did it anyway.

"I know I have no right to complain, Mr. Elkins," I said, "and I know I have every reason to be grateful to you. And I am, sir. I truly am. But the fact of the matter—and I mean this with all due respect—is that in the office of the mayor of Bloomington, Indiana, a town that I realize is one-hundredth the size of L.A., I worked on position papers and citywide issues. I had daily contact with the mayor, and if I may say so, I had a positive impact on her administration. I think I can do that for this administration as well. I'm here for only one short semester, but being isolated on the twenty-second floor is frustrating and isn't taking advantage of my skills. I hope you don't take offense at my speaking my mind, sir."

"I wouldn't expect anything else from you, Tavis."

"It's just that I feel like I'm being wasted, Mr. Elkins. I don't think I've been given enough to do, and what I have to do can be done in an hour's time."

"So you want to be kept busy with important work?"

"I think I could be helpful to you and the mayor," I said.

"I'll give careful thought to all this, Tavis."

"And I'd like to mention one other thing, Mr. Elkins."

"Feel free."

"I'd like to have face time with the mayor. I'd like to see how he works, and I'd like to help him do that work."

"Tavis," said Elkins, shaking his head and chuckling under his breath, "if you don't know the meaning of *chutzpah*, you'd better look it up."

After I looked up *chutzpah* and found that it was a Yiddish word meaning "nerve" or "impudence," I expected either to be thrown out on my butt or to be given greater responsibility. Fortunately, I was given greater responsibility. Everything shifted after my talk with Elkins. He took my request and my chutzpah in the right spirit. He saw my desire to help. Elkins was another angel in my life, the kind of angel who helps people move along the right path at the right time.

Elkins called me into his office a week later. "Tavis," he said, "the mayor came up with a plan that should make you happy. No, he hasn't decided to resign and name you to his post as mayor—you'll have to wait a few more years for that to happen—but he has decided to put you on the detail for planning the city's first celebration of Martin Luther King Jr. Day."

I was flabbergasted and flattered. This was what I'd been dreaming of—a plum assignment. Even better, it was an assignment with personal meaning. What better task than to work on ways to publicly honor my hero? I knew the history: Four days after Dr. King was assassinated in 1968, Congressman John Conyers initiated legislation to honor Dr. King with a day of his own. Fifteen long years later, after endless stalling and squabbling, the bill was finally signed into law by President Reagan. The third Monday of January 1986 would mark the first day of the annual Dr. Martin Luther King Jr. holiday. "The city of Los Angeles," said Elkins, "in conjunction with the Los Angeles chapter of the Southern Christian Leadership Conference, wants to create a celebration that will highlight the permanent relevance of King's work while attracting widespread media attention."

I was put on a team responsible for bringing Nobel laureate Desmond Tutu to lead our celebration. We worked feverishly to make it happen. And on that day, marked with prayer breakfasts, meetings, and gala banquets, I was among those to meet with Bishop Tutu and escort him to the events. As a result of everyone's hard work, the first annual Martin Luther King Jr. Day in Los Angeles went off without a hitch.

I knew that Mayor Bradley noticed me and, I'd like to believe, appreciated my drive. He let me in on meetings no intern had ever been privileged to attend; he asked me to explore, in research and policy papers, citywide issues. All my hopes and dreams of working with Mayor Bradley were being realized. Not only was I dealing with important matters, I was getting to know the mayor personally. I loved the man.

A former track star, Bradley was rock steady, a leader with a ready smile and uproarious sense of humor. When he laughed, his entire upper body rocked back and forth. I was in awe of his political skills. While I respected Coleman Young in Detroit and Harold Washington in Chicago, black mayors of tremendous achievement, those cities had huge black populations. Blacks constituted only 13 percent of Los Angeles, and yet Bradley had won the heart and trust of the community. Moreover, he was one of the first black mayors of a major U.S. city since the civil-rights movement.

I also loved and learned from Bradley's style. He was a minimalist in terms of pomp and circumstance. He had no entourage, just one guy who drove him around while he, the mayor, sat in the front seat. He was as far from being a media hog as any politician I've ever observed. When I once pointed out an event that would garner great publicity, he said, "Tavis, I get enough of that. I'd rather my work speak for itself." How many politicians act according to that creed?

Bradley's work ethic reminded me of Daddy's. Like the Smileys, the mayor came from meager means. The grandson of slaves and son of sharecroppers, he worked tirelessly for the people. "This is a gift," he once said to me, referring to his ability to lead, "and I don't intend to waste any of it." I remember watching him take off on a flight to Asia on a Monday. When he landed back at

LAX that Saturday at 11 A.M., he was in the office by noon, working a full day as if he'd been around the block, rather than around the world. Eighteen-hour days were normal. I kept up with him, but it took everything I had.

When my four-month internship was over, it also took everything I had to go into the mayor's office and tell him something I knew would not make him happy.

"Mr. Mayor," I said, "I can't go back to college."

"Why is that, Tavis?" he asked.

"I love this job, Mr. Mayor. I'm hooked on it. It's too exciting for me to leave. Nothing can compare to the challenges you've given me. I don't see how I can go back to Indiana."

"I don't see how you can *not* go back," he said. "You need that degree, son."

"I'll get my degree, Mr. Mayor. Eventually."

" 'Eventually' isn't good enough, Tavis. 'Eventually' is procrastination. 'Eventually' doesn't cut it."

"I think I can work out a plan with the university that . . ."

"Look, Tavis," the mayor said, stopping me in my tracks, "I know you're good at working out plans. You're the master of working out plans. But this is one plan that doesn't need working out. The plan is already in place. You came here to serve an internship. You've done a superlative job. You've made certain your school will give you credit. That was good thinking, son. But now your thinking has to revert back to pure education. I couldn't stand aside and watch someone with your potential pass up the chance to complete your course work."

"I understand, Mr. Mayor, but I'm not sure that once I'm back at IU, I'll find the concentration needed to . . ."

"I know you, Tavis. You'll do what you need to do. Now, I'm afraid this discussion is over."

"Yes, sir."

I thanked the mayor for his time, but my head was hanging low, so low, in fact, that Mayor Bradley took a few steps back and gave me a once-over.

"Look, Tavis," he said, "I know this isn't easy for you. You've been a spark plug, and we'll miss you. I also know college isn't as exciting as the real world. But perhaps this will ease your mind: once you're out, I can promise you that you'll have a job waiting for you here."

With those words, my despair turned to euphoria. "That's great, Mr. Mayor," I said, gripping his hand. "Sir, that changes everything."

# Lame-Duck Hoosier

**M**aking my way back to Indiana wasn't easy. I was tired of that long drive, so I took the last of my money and bought my mother and brother plane tickets to Los Angeles. The plan was that they'd drive my Datsun back to Bloomington and I'd fly. The problem was that I lacked the cash to buy them gas and buy myself a ticket. Poor planning.

Time for more hustle and flow: I thought of the Indiana University alumni organization. By tapping their membership, could I find someone with a connection to L.A. city government? I could, and I did, a man who was a concessionaire at the Rose Bowl and a supporter of Mayor Bradley. I approached him gingerly, explaining how, as an unpaid intern, I was without funds and means to return to Bloomington. Could he lend me the money to get back? He wasn't open to lending me the money, but he was willing to let me hawk banners, balloons, T-shirts, and sweatshirts at the Rose Bowl and pocket whatever I sold.

That year, Arizona State beat Michigan by a touchdown, but I didn't see a second of the game. No one in the history of collegiate sports has peddled products with such exuberance. I couldn't be stopped. I was up and down the aisles, first on the Arizona State side, then on the Michigan side, my arms loaded with pennants and caps, mementos of every stripe, my mouth working nonstop—"Get your genuine souvenirs here! Get your once-in-a-lifetime souvenirs here!"—until my throat was raw and my voice hoarse. But every last piece of merchandise was sold. My total take was seven hundred dollars, enough to get Mama and my brother back to Bloomington by car and me a coach seat on the red-eye.

I always had a plan in those days. Still do, in fact. My back-in-Bloomington plan involved finishing up college in a year, taking the LSAT for law school, going to work for Mayor Bradley the following January, and attending Harvard Law School the following fall. I felt sure the plan would work. During my internship in L.A., I had met and befriended Claude Pepper, the famous congressman from Florida who had championed the rights of the elderly. Pepper was a distinguished graduate of Harvard Law and promised to help me get in. We corresponded over the next year on a wide variety of political issues; I knew I could count on his recommendation. Beyond that, my bid to continue my work-study program, this time in the office of the chancellor of the university, had been accepted.

Yet even with my plan in place, I was hit with a severe case of the blues. Why? How could I be depressed? I was viewed as a hero at IU, someone who'd worked for the great Tom Bradley. I was the guy who'd hung out with Jim Brown, Magic Johnson, and Bishop Tutu.

The truth was that I was bored with school. The truth was that once this boxcar child had gotten a look at L.A., it was hard to get him back in the boxcar. I'd taken a bite out of the Big Orange, and the taste was sweet. I couldn't get that taste out of my mouth. School seemed irrelevant, slow, abstract. The world of politics was real. Professors dealt with theory; politicians dealt with the practical. I felt like I'd moved beyond college. I just couldn't get my head into my books.

Somehow I plowed through. I took the LSAT. I didn't do great the first time; the second time I did a little better. My courses still bored me, but I consoled myself with the knowledge that I had a great job waiting for me. My friend Chi and I hung out with three seniors who were applying for jobs left and right. They weren't getting anywhere and decided to fashion their rejection letters into wallpaper. Soon their apartment was covered with no-thank-you wallpaper. They turned it into a joke. I admired their never-say-die spirit. Getting work was no easy feat, and the fact that I had done so before anyone else should have brought me comfort. Unfortunately, it didn't. My body was in Bloomington, but my mind was in L.A.

I couldn't wrap my mind around a required computer class. I can type proficiently, but computers have never interested me. Without a passing grade in this pass-fail course, though, I couldn't graduate. So I took it, but gave it minimal attention.

During our first test, the teacher, a female graduate student, said, "Please keep your eyes on your own paper." I presumed she was talking to the entire class and thought nothing of it. Teachers say that all the time. When she returned our papers during the following class, I saw she had written an A– on mine, but underneath it, larger, was an F followed by the words, "Keep your eyes on your own paper."

I immediately shot up my hand.

"Yes, Mr. Smiley."

"My paper says A–, but then there's this F."

"Read the note under the F."

I read it aloud. It said I had been copying.

"That should be self-explanatory, Mr. Smiley."

"Well, it's not."

The class laughed at me. That made me angrier. "I'd like an explanation," I said.

"You were looking at your neighbor's paper. It's that simple."

But it wasn't that simple. She was wrong. I hadn't cheated. And her accusation triggered memories of the incident at church ten years earlier, when I was falsely accused. Only this time I would not go undefended. I was a debate champ. I was determined to give this graduate student a piece of my mind.

"First," I said to her in front of the class, "we're squeezed next to each other in this class like sardines, so it's impossible to turn your head or even pop your neck without it looking like something it isn't. Second, if you thought I was cheating you had an obligation to accuse me and stop me in what you considered the act itself. Furthermore, for all we know, you could accuse anyone in this classroom whom you happen to dislike. If you had an attitude about blacks, for example, what better way to express that than by accusing me of cheating."

Yes, I played the race card. My assault was stinging—so stinging, in fact, that the teacher ran out of the room in tears. The class broke out into applause.

I ran out of the room as well to beat her to the dean's office. I knew the dean well, and I explained my case to him. When I was through, I saw the computer teacher waiting in the dean's outer office. She and the dean met privately. When they were through, I was called in for a Come to Jesus meeting—me, the dean, and this graduate-student teacher.

"Tavis," said the dean, "I see your point and I do not believe this was handled in the proper manner. I'm going to take it upon myself to remove this F.

"At the same time, though," he added, "there are several other computer classes available, and I think it's best that you transfer into one of those."

"Dean, I don't think that's right," I argued. "I didn't do anything wrong. To ask me to rearrange my schedule implies that you've found fault with me when, in fact, you haven't. I should have every right to remain in the class and not be forced to rearrange my schedule so late in the semester."

"Well, if that's how you feel, Mr. Smiley . . ."

"I'm sorry, but I do," I said.

"So be it. You'll remain in the class."

And without so much as looking at the teacher, I left.

Weeks passed. My interest in the course waned. I missed several classes, and when it came to the final exam, I forgot most of what I had learned. I made a mess of the test and found that I had failed.

The failing grade shocked me. In my arrogant mind-set, I thought I had intimidated the teacher so much that she wouldn't dare flunk me. My arrogance had blinded me. Worse, the failing grade meant that I couldn't graduate. This was a required course, and without passing, I could not get into law school, no matter how powerful Congressman Pepper's influence. I had to tuck my tail between my legs and go to the teacher and beg for mercy.

"I understand I did poorly," I told her, "but please give me a D–. It would at least let me graduate and be considered for Harvard Law."

"Mr. Smiley," she said, "I know you're not asking me to give you a grade you didn't earn."

"No," I countered. "It's only that the distance between an F and a D– is minuscule. I'm just asking that you give a brother a break."

"I have a solution," she suggested.

"What is it?"

"Why don't we go to the dean and see what he has to say."

"Touché," I said, acknowledging defeat. I let the discussion die right there.

Beyond failing computer class, I did poorly in several other courses and lacked nine hours of credits to graduate. I could only graduate by staying a fifth year. That meant spending another winter in Bloomington. I just couldn't do it.

With L.A. calling, Indiana was history. Besides, my debate team scholarship was over, as were my Pell Grants. Beyond the four-year mark, you're on your own. My best bet was to cut my losses, forget law school for the time being, head west, and make up my credits through correspondence or community college. My best bet was still Mayor Tom Bradley.

I drove out to L.A. with Junebug, a friend from church, and ar-rived on a day of extravagant sunshine. At that time, you couldn't tell me I'd made the wrong move. I ran over to city hall and bumped into Bill Elkins, the very man I wanted to see.

"I was hoping I'd get an office on the third floor, not far from the mayor," I told him.

"I'm afraid there won't be any office, Tavis."

"What do you mean?" I asked.

"There is a hiring freeze for the entire government."

"For how long?"

"Indefinitely."

# Chillin' in the Deep Freeze

**M**y momentum was stopped cold. I needed forward motion; I needed to be working toward my goals; I needed to feel like I was moving up and making headway. Without that, I was singing the blues.

Two simple words—*hiring freeze*—had turned my jubilant mood to despair. The blues were all over me. It was the last thing in the world I expected. Emotionally and financially, I was unprepared to face unemployment. I'd spent my last year at IU dreaming of diving back into the mainstream of municipal action. As a member of Bradley's staff, my status would go up, my duties would expand, and I'd be paid. Now I had no pay, no status, no job.

Uncertainty and fear gnawed at me, the same fear I'd first faced when I spent that time in the hospital over a decade earlier. The public humiliation and its long aftermath still haunted me. It was as if I could never achieve enough to put the pain of that beating behind me. My thoughts turned bleak. It felt like darkness was just a step away, like I was in a footrace with shame and failure. I was convinced that I would wind up a nobody and would accomplish nothing. All those victories—my debate victories, my successes in high-profile jobs, my positions as student leader—were all but fleeting accidents. My real fortune, I felt deep at heart, was misfortune. My real path was anonymity and failure.

When times are tough, many of us hear such voices whispering in our heads. Especially when, week after week, we search for work and come up empty-handed. Maybe we all fall into self-recrimination when the cupboard is bare and the gas tank empty. Maybe the enemy—the destructive force whose job it is to keep us from our best selves—gains power when things go badly for us.

At least that was my condition as I searched for some kind of job, any kind of job, to see me through. L.A. is a great place when you've got work, when you're sitting pretty up in city hall. But from a one-room apartment in the hood, with the rent due and no money in your pocket, the city looks grim.

While buying a Big Mac that would serve as my meal of the day, I resigned myself to filling out an application to work at the McDonald's where I was eating. I handed it to the manager and sat around while he read it.

"Mr. Smiley," he said, "you are woefully overqualified for any work we might have."

"Woefully" was the right word. But "overqualified" was also the word they used at Burger King, Jack in the Box, and Arby's. I decided to apply for better jobs and did so through qualified headhunters. They sent me out to high-level interviews—administration posts, managerial positions—but there I was *under*qualified. I was falling through all the cracks, and in the meanwhile, I was eating beans and living on frozen dinners. When they turned off my electricity, I was back to beans.

My landlord sent me a third notice about my overdue rent.

Only this time she used the word *eviction*. "You have forty-eight hours to pay," she said, "or else you must move out."

My friend Harold Patrick, a successful businessman whom I had met through Mayor Bradley, offered to lend me the money, but I was already in debt to Harold. Besides slipping me two or three hundred dollars from time to time, Harold and his wife often had me over for dinner and paid me to baby-sit their two young kids. Harold was the big brother I never had. But I couldn't continue living off his goodwill. For weeks now, I had been certain that something would break. But nothing came through, nor were there any prospects on the horizon. As Gladys Knight and the Pips pointed out, L.A. was proving "too much for the man." I was about to get on the midnight train to Kokomo. I called Mama to make sure my room was ready.

"Your room is always ready, baby," she said. "You come home whenever you want. The Lord is with you wherever you go. The Lord is protecting you whatever you do. And if you listen to the Lord, you'll know what to do."

I love Mama more than life itself, but I had the distinct feeling that the Lord talked to Mama a lot more than he talked to me. I hadn't heard a word from him in a while. But I did hear from my friend Harold.

"Give yourself another week, Tavis," he urged. "This whole thing could turn around in a week."

"I don't have a week," I said. "I'm about to get thrown out of my apartment."

"Then you'll come live with us," Harold offered.

"I appreciate that, Harold, and I love you and your family, but what good will that do?"

"It'll be warmer than the streets."

"I think I'm going home to Indiana."

"Whatever your decision, I'm behind you, Tavis. But I really do believe you'll do great things in Los Angeles. I think this is your city. You just need to give it more time."

I looked at the single can of Franco-American SpaghettiOs that I planned to have for dinner and said, "Time's run out, Harold."

That was a Tuesday night. I planned on leaving the city for Kokomo on Wednesday. Thursday was eviction day. But because of Harold's plea, I decided to give it another twenty-four hours. I'd stay Wednesday and leave Thursday.

I was in the shower Wednesday night, dreading the act of packing when I heard a voice say, "As long as you're alive, there's hope. It can always get worse. Hang in." I looked around the shower to see if someone had installed a speaker. I wondered if someone was piping in a recording. Was this a joke? It wasn't. I had heard what I heard.

Next morning, instead of packing, I made myself a bowl of cornflakes and read the paper. At ten o'clock, the phone rang. It was Bill Elkins.

"Congratulations, Tavis," he said. "The city-government freeze has been lifted. Consider yourself a paid full-time employee of Mayor Bradley's staff."

I could go into the lessons learned about patience and tenacity, but I think you get the picture. Just when I thought I had been patient and tenacious enough, I learned I needed to be even more patient, even more tenacious.

# End of the Eighties

As Ronald Reagan moved out of the White House following his second term and President-elect George Bush trounced Michael Dukakis to take Reagan's place, I was once again in city hall, a young man on the rise.

When I'm busy, I'm happy, and fortunately the mayor kept me busy. He named me one of six people in charge of various sections of the city. My section was South L.A. I oversaw some twelve zip codes and acted in the role of a junior mayor. Any community problem came to me. If I could handle it, I would. If I couldn't, I'd take it to the mayor. The responsibility was heavy, and I loved it. For a couple of years I worked my tail off, raising my profile in the community and learning the ins and outs of running a big area of a big city. I was the eyes and ears of South L.A. I was also virtually autonomous and, as time went on, gained even more of Tom Bradley's trust.

But it all changed overnight when the mayor appointed a thirty-something white boy from Harvard as his new deputy mayor.

First thing the deputy mayor did was break up Bradley's structure of junior mayors. I lost my autonomy, lost my section of the city, lost my city car, my secretary, and even my office in the mayor's suite. I was shipped back up to the twenty-second floor, where I'd started out as an intern! I felt as if I'd been sent to Siberia.

For a while I tried to convince the deputy mayor that I was being underused, but he took little notice of me. I realized I had no choice but to go to Mayor Bradley himself. Bradley was a nonconfrontational kind of guy, a born diplomat who loathed disputes. It was because of that that he avoided me during this period of unrest. I understood his style—I respected his style—but I also had a point to make. When I couldn't get a meeting with him, I wrote a letter and slipped it under his door. The letter was an impassioned argument that I return to my former position.

Finally the mayor agreed to see me. I poured out my heart and found him sympathetic. "But at the same time, Tavis," he said, "I don't want to undercut the deputy mayor's authority. What I will do, though, is give you back your city car." That was it. I didn't regain my office on the mayor's floor, my secretary, or what mattered most to me, my responsibility over South L.A. I was still stuck in Siberia.

Enter Magnificent Montague, the famous disc jockey immortalized not only for his trail-blazing radio personality but also his coining the phrase "Burn, baby, burn!" Montague was also the black Jack LaLanne, an older brother in better shape than dudes one-third his age. Montague and I became friends during my time in L.A., and it was Montague who said the words I needed to hear. "Bradley's cool, Tavis," he said, "but believe me, brother, you got to chart your own course."

Montague was right.

Mayor Bradley was terrific. He had changed my life and given me opportunities that were unparalleled. But in some ways, Mayor Bradley was holding me back. Or more to the point, I was holding myself back. I needed to move on, and my next step had to be big and bold. I needed to catapult myself into a whole new arena.

The next step, I decided, was to enter elective politics.

At twenty-six, I decided to run for city council. Given my drive and experience, I felt there was no way I could lose.

# I Lost

In spite of a vigorous campaign, I didn't even make the runoff. Everyone said that for a newcomer I did well, but I didn't want to hear that. I just wanted to go off and hide. All I knew was that I had given it all I had, and all I had wasn't enough. There was no way to sugarcoat defeat. The taste was bitter.

After any unsuccessful political campaign, there's a natural letdown. So much energy has been expended, so much hope generated, so many expectations dashed. On the other hand, there were reasons to feel good about my respectable showing. My district had been gerrymandered. The white population was larger, and the white turnout invariably trumped the black turnout. The district had never elected a black. The incumbent I opposed had greater resources. The mayor wouldn't make an endorsement, although he did arrange for his treasurer to become the treasurer of my campaign, a move that let everyone know that Bradley looked favorably upon my campaign. Despite this, our resources dwindled. One night, I told my mother that my funds had been exhausted.

"You know what, Tavis," she said, "I'm going to do something about that."

"What can you do, Mama?" I asked.

"Mortgage this house, that's what I can do."

"The house is all you got, Mama."

"God is all I got, son, and God is all I need. And I know that the Lord wants me to put my children before my own welfare."

"If you don't pay back that money, they'll foreclose on you."

"There's no foreclosing God, Tavis."

"I love you for the offer, Mama, but I don't want you to do it."

For all Mama's generosity, for the generosity of so many friends, the loss was still crushing. Or perhaps even more crushing because so many folks worked so hard for me. I felt like I'd let them down. So what was I to do now? Going back to city hall wasn't an option. Some high-up officials in the mayor's administration saw me as too ambitious. I resented that, especially when a number of the white members of Mayor Bradley's staff would eventually secure positions in the Clinton administration. Nothing irritated me more than to be accused of being a pushy Negro. It seemed as if whites can push as hard as they please, but somehow determination and drive are not seen as legitimate components of a black American's character.

I decided to seek the executive directorship of the Southern Christian Leadership Conference of Los Angeles. Mark Ridley-Thomas had held the post before, but, running in a different district than me, Mark had won a council position in the same general election I had lost. His position as head of SCLC was vacant. I had been assured, having at one time worked with Mark, that I'd be a shoo-in. I was young—still only twenty-six—to hold such an office, but Mark had been that very age when he was chosen executive director. So I decided to go for it. It was, after all, the organization cofounded by Dr. King and a high-profile position that would tap my skills as a planner and politico. Besides, there seemed to be no competition.

A competitor, however, soon emerged. The competitor, I was told, wouldn't be able to match my qualifications. But when a member of the selection committee backing my competitor insinuated to his colleagues that I had had issues with manipulating money, I lost the contest. To ensure my defeat, the man straight-out lied, slamming my reputation. It cost me the job.

Two very public defeats, one after the other.

How could I praise God at a time like that?

How could I stay positive?

## Just a Thought

When I called Mama, she said, "God is there. God is everywhere. God is faithful even when your faith might weaken."

Big Mama told me the same thing. "You might think God's gone away. You might think we've been deserted. But God is in the bad as well as the good. The bad is what lets us love the good. And God is what lets us love life, even when life ain't going our way."

"Your defeats," said my friend Harold, "are just setting you up for bigger victories."

Whatever challenges God meted out to me, he also surrounded me with loving people. Their praise renewed my spirit and gave me energy. My fear of failure couldn't counteract the power of that energy. I was determined to turn the fear into energy.

I needed to return to practical considerations, such as finding a job. I needed money to live, and as someone who wanted to win elective office, I needed to keep my name before the public. I also needed a forum to discuss public issues.

A job that satisfied those three needs didn't seem to exist. So I did the next best thing—I invented a job. I became a radio commentator. I created something called *The Smiley Report*. At first, my "report" was nothing but a name. Stations were not prepared to hire me. Stations, in fact, were decidedly uninterested in what I had to say, off or on the air.

But at one AM station, KGFJ, the manager was intrigued. "I'll put you on the air," he said, "but only if you find your own sponsor." That got me to thinking about a woman I'd worked with when I was in the mayor's office, Wendi Chavis. She was in charge of an urban-outreach program for a big bank. Wendi came through, and the bank underwrote my one-minute radio commentary. I called it "Just a Thought." KGFJ put me on during morning drive time, five days a week, where I discussed everything from gun control to abortion. Soon the commentary caught on, and I was given an additional spot in the afternoon.

Next thing I knew, Stevie Wonder heard me and had me on his FM station, KJLH. From there I went to a huge urban station called The Beat. Not long afterward, the most amazing offer of all came in: channel 7, the ABC affiliate and number-one station in the L.A. market, asked me to take my commentary on TV during their five o'clock news.

To their surprise, however, I said no.

My decision surprised even me. It seemed like an offer I couldn't refuse. So why did I?

With the good advice of friends, I saw I wasn't ready. I had never been on camera and didn't know the first thing about it. I reasoned that if I plunged into television without proper preparation, I might not be given a second chance. So I respectfully declined. Then I swung into action.

I hooked up with a local cable outfit on Crenshaw Boulevard

in the heart of black L.A. It was a makeshift operation, but it was beautiful. None of us knew what we were doing; we made mistakes, but encouragement was our way of making it through. I was put on a program of community news and stayed on the air for six months, learning my craft. Staring into a camera became a little less intimidating.

For the next six months, I managed to find work on television in Montreal, Canada. It was more woodshedding: how to read a TelePrompTer, how to breathe, enunciate, and find that elusive zone between being relaxed and being alert. I moderated a news panel and grew more comfortable in my own skin.

When I got back to L.A., I called up channel 7 and asked them if the commentator position was still open. It was.

"May I audition?" I asked.

"Yes," they replied. "Come in tomorrow morning."

I showed up on the set bright and early, my suit pressed, my shoes shined.

"You want a practice read-through, Mr. Smiley?" the producer asked.

"No," I said, "I'm ready to roll."

With the very first reading, I nailed it.

"You got the job," the producer told me.

And the next week I was on the air.

I also got my job back at The Beat, but gave it up when KABC radio, the biggest talk station in California, offered to put on my commentary. Suddenly I was on the number-one TV news show and the number-one radio talk show in Los Angeles. The *Los Angeles Times* ran an article on me. *Time* magazine called and included me in a cover story called "Fifty for the Future" about the leaders of tomorrow.

"Mama!" I shouted over the phone. "I'm in *Time*!"

Mama ran out, bought the magazine, and called back.

"I don't see your name," she said.

"Look again," I urged.

"Oh, there you are, Tavis. I didn't know you had to share the honor with all these other people."

"Mama, you could hardly expect *Time* to mention only me."

"I'd expect nothing less, son."

I compiled my commentaries and, together with Denise Pines, who still works with me, self-published my first book, *Just a Thought*. I parlayed that book into a deal with a major publisher that led to my first full-length book, *Hard Left*. That brought even more national exposure.

My friend Ron Brown had become Clinton's secretary of commerce. Brown told President Clinton about me, and in 1996 the Clintons invited me to the White House. I was thirty-one years old, and I found myself being asked to give black-media-outreach advice to the president about the upcoming reelection.

It was at that White House meeting that I first met Tom Joyner, the nationally syndicated radio personality. Tom and I immediately clicked. He later read *Hard Left*, agreed with its politics, and invited me to join his show as a regular commentator. Tom's passion for public advocacy was as great as mine. In the 1996 election we ran a voter-registration drive, identifying six cities where worthy black candidates faced close elections. In each of those cities, we put on a concert of music guaranteed to draw a crowd. Admission was free, but only for those with proof of voter registration. The drive was a tremendous success, and all our candidates won.

It seemed like everything was working for me. Together, Tom and I were trailblazers on a number of issues, forcing advertisers who discriminated against minority media to recant and change their policies. Finally, I was able to put my demons behind me. My public humiliations seemed to become a thing of the past. I had entered a land where success seemed to be writ large on my future. I thanked God and breathed a sigh of relief.

Little did I know, my next move to national television would be not only the biggest move of my life but one that would also lead to the most painful public humiliation of all.

# A Good Bet

As businessmen and -women, black folk have nothing against capitalism. We'd just like to get more of the *capital* and less of the *ism*: racism, sexism, cronyism.

Because it's been so tough for black Americans to make their way inside the world of American capitalism, I have special appreciation for men like John H. Johnson, who built a publishing empire with *Ebony* magazine and, at the same time, served the African American community. That's why I respected the concept behind BET, Black Entertainment Television, as a means to inform and uplift black people.

When BET contacted me in the mid-1990s to audition for a late-night talk show, however, I wasn't interested. I was busy doing television and radio in L.A.; I was also doing national commentary with Tom Joyner. The idea of picking up and moving to Washington, D.C., BET national headquarters, held little appeal. Besides, the network was unclear about the kind of show they wanted. They seemed to be grasping at straws. Moreover, their auditioning process was bizarre. Their plan was to test a dozen hosts. Each would be given a week on the air. At the end of the twelfth week, a winner would be declared. I didn't like this system and decided not to participate.

"But, Tavis," my agent prevailed, "they'll fly you out first-class, give you a per diem, put you up at a fancy hotel, and pay you for the week. Besides, if they don't choose you, you'll have a week of tape hosting a talk show. Eventually, you will want a show of your own, and the tape will help you get it. See my point?"

"I do."

"Good," she continued, "but I have another point. All the other candidates for host—"

"By the way," I broke in, "who are the other candidates?"

"Everyone from Ice T to Snoop Dogg. None of those candidates wants to go on first, and BET is having fits trying to figure out the order of appearance."

"Just tell them I'll go first."

"You will?"

"If I'm good, they'll know about it in a hurry. If I bomb, so be it. I'd rather know sooner than later."

And so on Friday, September 13, 1996, my thirty-second birthday, I flew to Washington, D.C., to prepare to host my first show that coming Monday. When the plane landed, I learned that Tupac Shakur had died. It was yet another instance when the death of someone important to me occurred on my birthday—and indirectly upended my life. My first guest on the show was going to be Whitney Houston, but Tupac was on all our minds. BET urged me to postpone Whitney and plan a show around Tupac. I agreed. We scrambled to line up prominent guests like Chuck D and rap entrepreneur Russell Simmons. Monday evening I went on the air. The show was called *BET Talk*.

I did commentary on Tupac's importance in hip-hop history, as well as interviews with several of his colleagues. Russell Simmons was due at our affiliate in the Los Angeles studio and scheduled to be the final interview. But Russell was being difficult. He was late, casually having dinner at a Melrose Avenue hot spot. My producers called him and cajoled him into getting in the limo. When he arrived at the studio, though, he refused to get out of the backseat, where he was horsing around with friends. The producers cajoled him some more, but to no avail. They banged on the darkened limousine window, but the window wouldn't open. When the window finally did roll down, Russell stuck his head out and said, "I'll do the interview on my cell phone."

I was stuck—I had no choice. We put up a still photo of Russell as I began speaking to him on his cell phone. The entire scene was ridiculous. Russell was sitting outside the studio, but he wouldn't go on camera.

"Mr. Simmons," I asked him, "I wonder, how much greater an artist Tupac could have become had he lived? I know he went through various stages of his life and career. Sometimes he was confused and conflicted. Given his genius for language, do you—"

"You house nigger," Simmons barked.

"Excuse me," I said, stunned.

"You heard me. You're a house nigger. You know how many interviews I turned down today? I'm giving my only Tupac interview to BET 'cause I figure BET will honor him, and you start talking this stuff. You're a house nigger, and I'm done. I'm outta here."

With that, Simmons hung up.

All of this happened live on the air, during my first night of hosting.

"We're going to take a break here," I told the audience. "Stay with us."

During the break, I took several deep breaths. Following the break, I said, "Welcome to the premiere of *BET Talk* with, as Russell Simmons has characterized me, America's favorite house nigger."

It would take two years for me to dig my way out of Russell Simmons's accusation and prove myself to the hip-hop community. Getting major rappers on my show was no easy feat.

In spite of that nightmarish beginning, the first week went extremely well. On Friday, after the fifth and final taping, I flew back to L.A. The next morning, my agent called to say, "BET wants you to fly back."

"To D.C.?"

"They want you to do another week."

So I unpacked, repacked, flew back, and did another week. And another. And another after that. After twelve weeks, BET offered me a permanent post as host. No one else was ever auditioned. BET was infamous for its inferior pay, so I was astonished when they met my terms. I received a compensation package worth a half-million dollars, the biggest in BET history.

# The Press and the President

A t BET, my ambition kicked into high gear. Every night I faced a national audience. I wanted to be a great host, bringing stories that informed and inspired my African American audience. I loved my people deeply; they were family. But I also had never abandoned the idea of public advocacy. From the start of my television career, I saw that I'd be walking a thin line between being a journalist and being an advocate. I wanted to be both. I tried to accomplish this, deciding that to be an advocate for humanity in the field of journalism meant asking questions others wouldn't, raising issues others avoided, profiling people others ignored. I wanted to explore the times in which we lived, while shedding light on the dark corners of the national and international stage.

My show on BET, in fairly short order, made me a household name in black America. And it helped me develop a strong relationship with the most powerful man in the world at that time, President William Jefferson Clinton.

During the Clinton administration, I was granted, along with Jim Lehrer of PBS, the largest number of presidential interviews of any TV journalist. Clinton's staff told me that whenever the president wanted to test a news story, he'd say, "Let's talk to Tavis. Let Tavis roll it out." He took that position, he claimed, not because I favored him but because he was convinced I'd treat him fairly. It was a useful way for him to test the waters. It's also fair to say something that most everyone in the country recognized: Clinton had rapport with the black community. He identified with us and championed our causes. He did so imperfectly, and at times I vociferously criticized him for what I perceived as wrong policy. In his heart, though, Clinton was as black a president as this country has ever known.

To illustrate that point, let me jump ahead to the funeral service for John H. Johnson, the founder and publisher of *Ebony* magazine, in 2005. Mr. Johnson, whom I admired as one of the great entrepreneurs in our history, began his empire on a five-hundred-dollar family loan. I recognized him as an elder touched by the same drive that drove me. When I was asked to speak at his funeral service in a magnificent chapel at the University of Chicago, I was honored. President Clinton, out of office for several years, was also in attendance.

In my remarks, I stressed Mr. Johnson's "any way" philosophy. To serve black folk, he began a magazine *any way*; he was going to make it in a white-dominated media world *any way*; he bought his own building on Michigan Avenue *any way*. "Any way is the only way we make our mark in this country," I said, "a fact that every black leader here today—and that includes you, Mr. President—knows full well." With that comment, the congregation rose to its feet and gave Clinton a thunderous ovation.

When the service was over, I was speaking with several leaders when Reverend Al Sharpton approached me.

"Your joke wasn't funny, Tavis," he said.

"What joke?"

"That Clinton is black. Problem with you people is that you're so busy kissing white folks' behinds, you make it hard for the rest of us who have issues with these so-called friends of ours. You give them a pass when they don't deserve it. What has this guy ever done for us?"

Sharpton was being loud and brassy in his remarks, and believe me, I wanted to be loud in response. But instead I thought of Mama and Big Mama, who were always advocating restraint.

"Are you finished, Reverend Sharpton?" I asked him.

"I am."

"Fine. I hope to continue this discussion in a more appropriate setting. Today I'm here to honor Mr. Johnson."

And Sharpton walked away.

I wanted to defend myself, to cite the times I had criticized President Clinton's crime bill myself or Clinton's welfare-reform package. But I didn't. I had meant what I said—the day belonged to Mr. Johnson.


In March 1998, President Clinton made the first extended trip to sub-Saharan Africa by a U.S. president in more than two decades. I was invited along with a delegation that included a large number of black leaders. We went to Botswana, Ghana, Rwanda, Senegal, Uganda, and South Africa. Before we reached Africa, though, a question raged among us—should President Clinton apologize for America's history of slavery at the Door of No Return on Senegal's

Gorée Island, the symbolic point of departure for millions of slaves sold into bondage? The debate went on and on to no resolution. That pained me, because it gave President Clinton an out: If black Americans can't decide how to advise me themselves, he reasoned, I'm off the hook to take bold action. When the president granted me an interview in South Africa, I saw he had made up his mind *not* to offer what would have been a historical apology. I pressed him on the issue and, back home, in one of my commentaries, sharply criticized him for his lack of sensitivity. I certainly wasn't afraid to take him on when I felt he'd fallen short.

Despite my criticism, six months later Clinton granted me his only one-on-one interview about the Monica Lewinsky scandal. This was the first time he agreed to talk about the incident with a journalist on the record. Of course, I was flattered. But I also understood his reasoning. The interview was set for a Monday, to be aired that night. The ratings would be huge. The timing was critical for Clinton because midterm elections took place the next day. With impeachment proceedings only two weeks away, he desperately needed to pick up Democratic seats to bolster his support. He needed to consolidate his black base, and appearing with me on BET would help.

I pressed him hard that night. But he is such a masterful politician that he stayed on message: he regretted his action and was putting it behind him. Much as I tried, I couldn't extract anything new. His tactic of appearing before one of his loyal constituencies, though, paid off. Black turnout the next day was substantial, and the Democrats picked up several congressional seats. In the end, that didn't prevent his impeachment, but it certainly didn't hurt his cause when the Senate found him not guilty.

———

The great lesson that I learned in dealing with President Clinton was that I—that all of us—need not be intimidated by anyone, even when that person is the most powerful man in the world. I don't mean to imply that I wasn't pleased that Clinton knew my name and that we had a good relationship. I was (and I continue to have a good relationship with him). But in facing him inside the Oval Office, it never occurred to me to shy away from or shirk my responsibilities. I did what I had to do. As human beings, we were equals. He simply had his job and I had mine.

In my job—confronting important world leaders with questions vital to Americans and particularly to the black community—I would take on even greater challenges. But I told myself there wasn't anyone who could scare me off. Confronting President Clinton, I thought, was the biggest test I could face.

I was wrong. A bigger test awaited me, only ninety miles off the coast of Florida.

# Castro

As a journalist and advocate, I've followed what many in the media would see as a nonconventional path. But looking back, I guess that's been true of everything in my life. There's a lesson in that. When there are no obvious paths to achieve your dreams, make up your own.

I had to do just that in my pursuit of major interviews. BET lacked the prestige and resources to attract international leaders. If I wanted to get a story or profile the head of a foreign government, I would often be on my own. That's why I wasn't averse to traveling with delegations. They were often the only way for me to get in.

That was the case in traveling to Cuba. I agreed to go with the TransAfrica Forum, a group whose mission is to influence United States policy on Africa and the Diaspora. In 1999, led by Randall Robinson, the man who marshaled the stateside fight in tearing down apartheid in South Africa, our delegation, which included Camille Cosby, Walter Mosley, and Danny Glover, went on a seven-day fact-finding trip to Cuba. It was the fortieth anniversary of Castro's Communist revolution. Randall, who was writing an article "Why Are Black Cubans Suffering?," was promised a meeting with Castro. I was told that I could video the meeting and conduct an interview. But the meeting with Castro kept getting postponed, day after day. By our final night, we had given up hope. We had an early plane out the next day. I was reconciled to the fact that Castro had neither the time nor the interest to meet with us. I was in bed when the call came. Castro wanted to see us. Now. As the youngest member of the delegation—the others called me "the kid"—I jumped into my clothes and ran down the hallway, banging on everyone's door. "Castro wants to see us! Castro wants to see us!"

In the dead of night, we were whisked to a palace where the Cuban dictator was waiting. We were ushered into a conference room. My cameraman was ready. Fifteen minutes later, Castro arrived. I found him to be one of the most charismatic figures I've ever encountered. Fidel Castro was larger than life, larger than the island of Cuba. By this time Castro had survived presidents Kennedy, Johnson, Nixon, Ford, Carter, Reagan, George H. W. Bush, and Clinton (and he would remain the head of Cuba while George W. Bush was in office). Dressed in fatigues, he hit the ground running. I asked perhaps three or four questions. It didn't take much, because once he started talking, there was no stopping him. His monologue went on for hours. His rambling, veering into propaganda, at times defied interruption or scrutiny. Moreover, the sound of his voice, even in a language I didn't understand—his words were instantaneously translated into English—was so hypnotic it was impossible to break through his breathless soliloquy. I managed to ask him about the recently relaxed travel restrictions from the United States to Cuba, and to that question I received a specific reply: He called them more symbolic than substantive.

After four hours, I politely stopped him. "Mr. President," I said, "I'm afraid we have to stop here. We're out of tape."

"What!" he exclaimed. "I'm just getting warmed up. I thought we'd have breakfast together."

"I wish we could, sir," I told him firmly, "but our plane leaves in an hour. Before we go, I'd like to ask you a favor."

"Please," replied Castro cordially.

"I'd be honored if you'd autograph this for me," I requested, handing him a photography book of Cuba. The pictures had been taken by Castro's personal photographer and the photographer's son.

Castro scrutinized the book intensely. "Where did you get this?"

"The publisher sent it to me."

"They didn't send a copy to me. I'd like to have this one."

"Well, sir," I said, "I'd love to accommodate you, but I'm afraid I can't. This is my only copy."

My fellow delegates looked at me like I was nuts. Their eyes said, *This is the dictator of Cuba you're talking to. We could be detained in Cuba indefinitely. Give the man the book.*

"I want this book," Castro insisted.

I hesitated, but I felt I had to stand my ground. "Sorry," I said.

"I'll send it to you in the United States as soon as mine arrives," said Castro.

"Mr. President, if I receive a package from Fidel Castro, my phone will be tapped for the rest of my natural life." *Besides*, I thought, *you'll never send the darn thing*.

He laughed but didn't relent.

"This book belongs in Havana before Los Angeles," he insisted.

"I understand your point of view," I said. "But it's my copy. May I ask you again for your autograph? It would mean a great deal to me."

A pregnant silence followed. No one said a word. And then President Castro said, "You are a stubborn man. But you are right, it is your book."

With that, he signed it, presented Camille Cosby with cigars for her husband Bill, and asked us into the next room for a group photo.

And an hour later we were on our way home.

# Big Mama

Our elders help get us through the difficult times. We need their insights, experience, and hard-earned sagacity. To deprive ourselves of their experience is foolish and self-defeating. Our elders are our teachers, our guides, our spiritual mentors; they offer advice and support when the world trips us up and circumstances confound our plans. For me, they have been a rock-steady support system, and as such, they are precious.

No elder has been more precious in my life than Big Mama. When it came to spirituality, Big Mama was the bottom line—always there, always true, always loving. She taught me an infinite number of lessons about how to live my life. But there were also some moments of high comedy. On one occasion in particular, however, Big Mama wasn't laughing—she was panicking on my behalf.

Frail and using a walker by this time, she was living with my mom, who never failed to watch me whenever I was on TV. That morning I was on television debating Jack Kemp, conservative congressman and Bob Dole's vice presidential candidate. Kemp is smart, a former Buffalo Bills quarterback who relishes verbal combat. I do too, so our exchange was sharp and even caustic. As our heated dialogue went on, back in Kokomo Big Mama made her way into the kitchen, where my mother was watching me on TV.

"Oh, my God," Big Mama said. "We gotta get in the car and get Tavis before they come after him."

"What are you talking about?" my mother asked.

"Our boy—he's sassing a white man. They gonna lynch him for that. We gotta get over there right away and hide him so he's safe."

"You don't understand, Mama. They pay Tavis to do this."

"*Pay* him to sass a white man?"

"Pay him good money."

"I don't believe it."

"Well, do you believe I'd be here relaxing with my tea if my son was in danger?"

"No."

"That's what I'm saying, Mama. There is no danger. Tavis can sass that man as long as he wants to. And he can sass him good, 'cause he's smarter than him and knows more about the subject. Just listen . . ."

Big Mama listened, shaking her head in amazement.

That night, after my mother reported the incident to me, I called Big Mama.

"I heard you were worried about me," I said.

"Child, I thought you were good as dead."

"Things have changed, Big Mama."

"Thank the Lord, Tavis. I just didn't think they had changed *that* much."

"In some ways they haven't, Big Mama. We can argue with the

white man in public, we can debate him on television, but he's still running things. We still have a long ways to go."

"But you're helping us get there, Tavis. I know you are. And you're going to arrive. I believe that in my soul."


February 18, 1999, was one of the saddest days of my life. That was the day Big Mama took her last breath. Her beautiful soul went over and joined the Lord's banquet. I flew home to be at her funeral.

I've been asked to speak at the funerals of many people, Ossie Davis and Rosa Parks among them. But none have mattered more to me than Big Mama. Speaking at her funeral was one of the greatest honors of my life.

"Big Mama was about life," I told those gathered at the service. "She had a great life force—a love for God and for Jesus—coursing through her spirit. But she was also well aware of the power and beauty of continuity. That's why she gave so much of herself to her children and grandchildren. She saw those coming after her as taking her place in the world, and she made our way easier. As Big Mama went home to God this week, at the very moment she breathed her last breath, God imbued a newborn with her first breath. Big Mama loved that sense of continuity. I believe that as she exited, an infant entered. My prayer is that infant will grow strong in faith like Big Mama grew strong in faith. I pray for the infant to assume the big-hearted character of Big Mama, the dignity, the grace, the joy, the compassion, the heart and soul for serving others. I pray that this child grows strong with the strength of Big Mama's determination and nurtures a family as Big Mama nurtured our family."

# Spring Thaw

Drive is a funny thing. I believe it has been the drive I've been blessed with, coupled with my work ethic, that has allowed me to excel in high school, to gain a college education when no clear path seemed to present itself, to win internships with mayors, and to prevail in the hotly competitive world of the media and public speaking. Ironically, I learned my work ethic from the same man whose savage beating of me helped shift my drive into high gear: my dad.

My attitude toward my dad was slow to change. For years, I felt fury over what had happened. Over time, the fury turned to smoldering anger and resentment. That was followed too often by cold indifference. Only when my dad first called to tell me that he and Mama were getting divorced did my heart go out to him and momentarily thaw. But the chill in our relationship soon returned. It was really only as an adult, when I had achieved a greater sense of security and success, that I could feel my heart softening. They say time is a great healer. But it doesn't work quickly. The time I needed to heal the hurt was the time it took me to grow from a boy to a man.

Today, I see the challenges of being a black male in America from a very different perspective. In time, I began to empathize with my dad's struggles and with the pressures to provide for his family and to earn the respect of those around him. I began to appreciate his hard-won accomplishments. I recognized how he had held our family together and how he had fought to maintain dignity in a white world where he felt himself disadvantaged.

Another factor contributed to my change in attitude. I was helped enormously by a man who became both my pastor and my friend, Bishop Noel Jones. He made a world of difference. Bishop Jones ministers his flock in Los Angeles, but so powerful was his message that almost every weekend while I was at BET I'd fly home to California from D.C. just to hear him preach. He never failed to offer a fresh word to his congregation, never failed to empower me. A friend of mine describes him as the "John Coltrane of evangelical preachers," referring to Bishop's original mind and the bold musicality of his message. Like me, Bishop comes out of a strict Pentecostal upbringing. He has his own issues with his dad. On that level and so many others, we related to each other immediately. His ability to overcome his past and infuse his ministry with love helped keep me connected. Bishop's faith deepened my faith. His powerful sense of possibility expanded my spiritual life. Inside me, I could feel old animosities begin to melt, like ice in a spring thaw.

One of the occasions of that thaw was a banquet I'd been invited to host honoring Muhammad Ali. I immediately thought of Daddy, as I did whenever I heard anything about Muhammad Ali. I thought of the times my father and I spent in front of the television watching the Greatest perform his magic. So when I received the invitation, I called my father.

"Dad," I said, calling long-distance, "I'd like you to accompany me to a special dinner."

As it turned out, he was thrilled by my call and even more thrilled to be seated with me near Ali. After the dinner and speeches, I found the right moment. I had interviewed Ali several times and knew him well. As I shook his hand, I said to him, "Champ, I'd like to introduce you to my father, Emory Smiley."

"It's a pleasure, Mr. Smiley," Ali said, looking at my father.

My dad could hardly speak; his eyes were filled with tears. The only other time I had seen him cry was at his father's funeral. But these weren't tears of sadness; they were tears of joy. His tears went far beyond any words he might have conveyed.

When the evening was over, Dad said to me, "Thank you, Tavis. I love you."

And finally, after all those years, my heart allowed me to say what I had always felt: "I love you too, Dad."

It was another lesson about bridging distances and allowing love to heal old wounds.

But as old wounds from my past finally began to mend, a new one—the most painful of my professional life—began to fester. I would need all my inner resources to get through it. The incident had the potential to destroy everything I had worked so hard to achieve. It took me by surprise and quickly became a national story.

# Final Bet

Despite the fact that my show at BET over the next four years was successful, the network remained wildly unorganized and understaffed. Moreover, BET was unwilling to venture into the all-important area of original programming. Instead, I was publicized as the poster boy for BET civic responsibility, although I sure didn't feel that way. The show had a political slant; for four years I interviewed everyone from the president to the pope. I snagged lots of exclusives along the way. But one show couldn't build up the ratings all alone. Bob Johnson, BET's owner, remained distant and remote. I had never, in fact, spoken in depth with the man.

It was in my fourth year when the storm touched down.

It began when *Newsweek* did an interview with me. In it, I said that although we had entered a new millennium, in my view, BET faced some challenges.

"Do you ever feel uncomfortable working for a network few

take seriously and others consider a joke?" the *Newsweek* reporter had asked me.

"I'm grateful for the opportunity BET has given me," I replied. "But I recognize that the network has issues. Since I'm an advocate by nature, I'd urge anyone with suggestions to write us. But as thankful as I am for my position, I cannot defend the network against all critiques. Many of those issues are legitimate."

When the issue of *Newsweek* with my interview came out, I found my remarks had been chopped up and rearranged to sound worse than they were. The essential point, though, that BET faced challenges as a network, remained clear.

Bob Johnson went ballistic.

I was in L.A. when he called me from Washington. He was at a staff meeting with some of his senior staff and had me on speakerphone.

"You disloyal son of a bitch," he said. "How the f— do you come off criticizing me in public? What gives you the audacity to say something negative about this network when this network has been paying you big money for years now? What the hell is wrong with you?"

And from there it got worse; the verbal abuse went on for several minutes. When he finally came up for air, I said, "Are you through?"

"For now I am."

"Good. And I assume, since we're both men here, I can communicate with you in the same manner you've communicated with me—without biting my tongue?"

"Go ahead."

"In the four years I've been working for BET, you've never called me once. Never had a one-minute conversation with me. Never sent me a single note or card. Never said 'Great show' after

I interviewed Clinton or Castro. You've never invited me to lunch. Never introduced me to your family. Now you call me up and cuss me out in front of a bunch of VPs. What kind of jerk are you? I watch Ted Turner on *Larry King*. They have a relationship, a friendship. Here I am, the highest-paid talent you have, and you don't give me the courtesy of a single word in four years, and now you feel you have the right to excoriate me. How dare you disrespect me this way! You can take this program and ram it up your black ass!"

To put it in the words of Cornel West, I was justified but not dignified.

I could hear the other executives gasp. No one talked to Bob Johnson this way. He was infamous for lashing out at his employees, but few had ever lashed back.

"Look," he said, mounting his defense, "I don't have relationships with my talent because I got a whole team that does that. I don't want my talent leapfrogging my executives to get to me."

"I'm not talking about a daily relationship," I said. "I'm just talking about the courtesy of a simple phone call from time to time."

"How can I put it so you'll understand it?" Johnson asked in his typically demeaning manner.

"Keep it simple," I said sarcastically, "and maybe I'll be able to grasp the basics."

"I see my on-air talent as parishioners. I see my executives as the pope. And I'm like—well, I'm like God. And you can't go past the pope to get to God."

Somehow I survived that first storm, but another soon gathered on the horizon.

My contract with BET allowed me to form my own production company. Through a set of fortunate circumstances, I was able to get an exclusive interview with Sarah Jane Olson, the Symbionese Liberation Army fugitive who had been apprehended after thirty years on the FBI's most wanted list. I spent my own money filming the piece, which was to be my first *60 Minutes*–style segment for network television. Because Sarah Jane Olson was a white soccer mom, it hardly seemed like the right segment for BET, which, in the interim, had been sold to Viacom. Viacom owns CBS, so we first went to CBS to sell the piece. But CBS wouldn't buy the segment because Dan Rather was chasing the Olson story himself. So ABC's *Prime Time Live* bought it instead. When it aired, it ran against CBS's new *Dragnet* TV series. *Prime Time Live,* featuring my Olson piece, beat the pants off *Dragnet,* and that infuriated Viacom.

Viacom demanded that Johnson explain what one of his boys was doing on ABC killing off their *Dragnet*. In typical fashion, Johnson didn't ask for an explanation from me. He never bothered to explain to the press that my news segment had been offered initially to CBS or that I had acted in conformity with my BET contract.

Instead, Johnson canned me. The firing was as public as public can be. The result was an uproar. My viewers came together and bombarded BET with angry letters and calls. The heat on Johnson was so intense that he had to perform damage control, appearing on TV for a full hour to take calls about my firing. The general consensus was that he made less than a brilliant case for himself and BET. Some six years later, my firing continues to be seen as one of the big blunders in BET history.

At the time, I didn't know that a rosier future was on the horizon. All I knew was that I had been canned, and I felt terrible.

Worse still, my firing had become national news. I had once again been humiliated. Being humiliated in the local newspapers in north central Indiana about a parental beating was one thing; this was coast-to-coast humiliation. This was BET-kicking-Tavis-to-the-curb humiliation.

My critics asked, "Is Tavis done? Is this the end for him?"

But somehow, somewhere inside me a voice affirmed, "No, this is the beginning."

# The Beginning

Today, I can look back and see the end of my BET career as a blessing in disguise. In fact, I'm grateful to Bob Johnson for firing me. Were it not for that turn of events, my life—spiritually and materially—would be much poorer. The firing freed me to go full circle in terms of the kind of journalism I was doing, free to reach out to everyone, regardless of color. No longer was I limited to one audience. I had always excelled in the media on network television; never did I view myself as someone who addressed the black community exclusively.

Just as significantly, my experience at BET convinced me to remain independent at any cost. Never again would I trust my career to a single organization. My dismissal made me realize that being an entrepreneur can serve a journalist as well as a businessman—and that the key to entrepreneurship was self-motivation, intelligent planning, and autonomy. The unrelenting work ethic I learned from my dad was another vital part of the equation. Smiley & Sons, in a different form and in a different medium, would always be part of my life.

In quick succession, I accepted deals with ABC, CNN, and National Public Radio (NPR). The ABC development deal, under the auspices of Buena Vista, had me develop a late-night interview show. For the pilot show, I managed to book Bill Gates, Bill Clinton, and Charlton Heston. But the show was beat out by *Jimmy Kimmel Live*. At the same time, I was a special correspondent for *Prime Time Live* and hosting and doing commentary for CNN. My first segment for *Prime Time Live*, in fact, was an interview with Will Smith and Muhammad Ali for the movie *Ali*. But it was with NPR that I developed the strongest relationship. There, five days a week over the next three years, I hosted *The Tavis Smiley Show*.

As an advocate-maverick, I felt that NPR would be perfect for me. I could address serious issues and help broaden the NPR base, reaching out to a relatively untapped audience of black listeners. I wanted to hire black producers, bookers, researchers, and support personnel. My first year began with a huge burst of energy.

My optimism was rooted in the belief that public conversations could unite our multiethnic society. I felt that public radio was the perfect forum to introduce Americans to one another by challenging listeners to reexamine their assumptions and expand their inventory of ideas. Sadly, it didn't take long for reality to undercut that optimism. A year into the venture, I saw that I was merely window dressing for NPR. When I pressed them to hire more black folk in key positions, they balked. They balked again when I campaigned to ambitiously and aggressively reach out to minority communities. It became evident that NPR was stuck in cement. In essence, it was a private club for educated white people, and I felt the network had no real interest in reaching beyond its core audience. Eventually, I got fed up.

There was another fallout from my NPR experience. It forced me to seriously reexamine myself and my mission. I saw that I was growing impatient in my job, as well as arrogant. I would have liked to ignore the truth behind this, but I couldn't. The proof was on a compact disc that showed me in the least favorable light.

It began when my producer made a mistake. The mistake was serious, but I overreacted, responding by ranting and raving. An engineer caught my temper tantrum on tape, made copies, and passed it around NPR. To put it in the words of Cornel West, here again my sentiments were justified but not dignified. I had embarrassed myself. I saw that my insistence on perfection and my intolerance of inefficiency had pushed me over the edge. My behavior was inexcusable. Faced with the CD, I couldn't deny the ugliness of my tone and the crudeness of my language. I decided not only to apologize but to stop cursing entirely, in any context, a bad habit I had picked up in college. The Tavis I heard throwing that fit was not the Tavis I wanted to be.

There was another blessing wrapped inside this lesson: Upon hearing the proof of my abusive behavior, I was determined to change myself and rise above this. Thank God, I realized later, that the engineer had made a tape.

Recognizing my culpability in my excessive behavior, though, and addressing it did not remedy my feelings about NPR. I remained convinced that the network was limiting my ability to reach out to audiences. And on a personal level, my schedule—getting to the studio every day at 3 A.M. to provide a live feed to the East Coast—was crushing. Rather than allowing myself to be crushed professionally and emotionally, I knew something had to be done.

Whenever I was suffering emotionally from a setback, whether in my personal life or my professional life, the person I turned to for support was my mother.

Three years before, at the time I left BET, I experienced a crushing personal setback as well. I had fallen in love with a special woman. Unfortunately, we lived in different cities. But we shared many wonderful trips and many beautiful weekends together. I had thought this was the woman I would marry. Work, though, seemed to always take precedence. Work seemed to rule my life.

And in the end, I lost her to another man. At the time, the emotional fallout was shattering. I cried over the loss of her every day. I spoke about us to my pastor, Bishop Jones. I spoke to my friends. I prayed to the Lord. I did everything to get over her. But nothing seemed to assuage the pain. The pain only seemed to worsen. On a rainy night in Georgia, I called my mom from an Atlanta hotel. I couldn't focus on anything but the woman I had lost.

"I hear you crying, Tavis," said Mama.

"The pain just doesn't stop," I admitted. "Nothing works. I can't think of anything but her. Mama, I can't handle it."

Hearing my pain, Mama began crying. Again, nothing upsets me more than to hear my mother cry.

"Why are *you* crying?" I asked through my depression.

"Because you've been crying for months now, Tavis. I just can't stand seeing you in such pain."

Miraculously, that's when my pain ended—when I saw what it was doing to my mother. From that day on, I managed to find a way to cope with my loss.

Mama has always been the bottom line in my life, even when I was rebelling against her. Without saying a word, Mama had let me know that there are things in life as important and worthwhile as my mission in life, my work. It was a simple lesson for most people, but unfortunately, because of the way I had been raised, it was not so simple for me. I get it now.

# Forces of Light

Of all the people who have been a part of my life, none has been more influential than my mother. As anyone who knows me well will tell you, I am my mother's son. Despite the tensions and differences, we are remarkably close in personality and spirit. She is an extrovert who expresses her opinion with extreme passion. I'm the same way. She has become an evangelist whose whole being is centered in Christ. I have inherited her faith in God and serve in my own way.

I've grown more excited about my mission to encourage, enlighten, and empower others over the years and have seen how closely this relates to Mama's mission. Our theology differs in important ways, but our determination is the same. My mother has more courage, conviction, and commitment than anyone I know. Because she believes liars will suffer damnation, she is absolutely committed to telling the truth, whatever the consequences. When she believes something, you cannot sway her or change her mind. And she will not compromise, whatever the setting. I remember two examples of her conviction. Both occurred on international television.

As part of my advocacy agenda, a number of years ago I began an annual broadcast on C-SPAN called "State of the Black Union." The event usually takes place in a black megachurch and features a wide range of leaders talking about a major subject in our lives. We reach an audience in the millions. This particular year, we focused on health in the black community. A number of prominent figures, gay and straight, spoke on the topic of sexuality and health. At the end of the conference, as usual I asked Mama, in her role as an evangelist, to give the closing prayer.

"Father God," she prayed before the church and the worldwide television audience, "we thank you for this opportunity to gather together and give you glory. We thank you, Father, for bringing in these leaders who have enlightened our minds with their thinking and their learning. But we also remember, Father, that you created Adam and Eve, not Adam and Steve, and so we pray that the practice of homosexuality be understood as the sin that it is. We pray that all your people turn away from sin and live a life pleasing to you. In Jesus' name, amen."

You could hear a pin drop. Without thinking twice, Mama took all the political correctness and tolerance that had been espoused and turned it on its ear. Some agreed with her; others were outraged. But discretion isn't part of Mama's vocabulary.

A year before, during the same annual broadcast, we conducted a raffle for a charitable cause. In the spur of the moment, I thought it would be a nice gesture to have my mother reach in and draw the winning ticket. This, too, took place live on C-SPAN.

"Now I will ask my mother," I said, "to honor us by randomly selecting the winner. Mama, if you will be so kind . . ."

Standing beside me in her lovely St. John suit, Mama looked

at me like I was crazy. For a second, I didn't understand. Then it hit me like a bolt of lightning: this was gambling. In Mama's view, gambling is immoral. I quickly had to reach in and draw the ticket myself.

"I can't believe it," a friend said to me the next day. "Boy, did your mama play you on national television! She made you look the fool."

But Mama wasn't concerned. Her conviction came first, even if it meant embarrassing her son before an audience of millions. That's what I call the gold standard of personal integrity and independence of thought.

At the end of 2004, I left NPR, following my own independent line of thinking. After three years, I knew our relationship was over. The friction between me and the suits at NPR had worn me down. I realized once again that the line I walk between advocacy and journalism is a lonely one. Most broadcast executives don't understand what I'm attempting to do. And because they sometimes make decisions based on ignorance, I don't always react well to their directives. For my part, I have complete confidence in what I'm doing, and being pushed off my path is frustrating.

In recent years, my life has consequently taken an even more independent turn. I created The Smiley Group, Inc., a holding company for my various interests; it gives me an entrepreneurial structure and a home base. It's my current version of Smiley & Sons. The Smiley Group is housed in a seven-thousand-square-foot office building/broadcast center on Crenshaw Boulevard in South Central Los Angeles, where I'm rooted in the neighborhood I love. Tavis Smiley Media handles my television, and Smiley Radio Properties handles radio productions. I'm proud to be the first journalist to have a daily show on both public radio and public television. And I've done so while retaining complete ownership of my programs.

Another branch of my company, Tavis Smiley Presents, is dedicated to planning and running major symposiums and forums on topics like economic prosperity, black health issues, and blacks in technology. Finally, I established the Tavis Smiley Foundation, a philanthropic agency devoted to cultivating leadership among young people.

None of this could have been achieved without the loyalty of a brilliant lawyer, Ken Browning, and a brilliant accountant, Errol Collier, who have been with me from the very beginning. What a blessing.

Our most recent "State of the Black Union" took place this year in Houston. It is one of the great blessings of my career. It was there that I presented *The Covenant with Black America*, a national plan of action to address the concerns of African Americans. A comprehensive 240-page document, *The Covenant* was written by some of the best black minds of our time, and covers everything from health to housing, crime to criminal justice, education to economic parity. As of this writing, the book has become a number-one *New York Times* bestseller, and is inspiring folk everywhere to use what is in it to shape their destinies and become forces of light in the world. And so my mission continues.

Among the deepest lessons I have learned growing up in America is, on one hand, to be grateful for all the many things we have: freedom, the potential to get ahead, the ability to achieve our dreams. At the same time, I know we must be tenacious in fighting for what we have yet to achieve: equal justice and education, economic opportunity for all. I am confident that the forces of light that Dr. King described will prevail. And I recognize the many gifts

I have been given. From my mother, I have been blessed with an abiding faith. From my father, I have learned that progress is made through hard work. Through faith and hard work, I believe, we can address any problem we choose to tackle.

So this is the essence of what I've learned growing up in America:

> *Have faith.*
> *Lasting change comes through hard work.*
> *And with faith and hard work, we can create an America as*
>     *good as its promise.*

# Index

# Index